# BETTY SHINE
## 1929–2002

Betty Shine was born in Kennington in 1929 and lived on the south coast. Betty was without doubt the most famous and influential medium alive. Highly respected for her remarkable psychic powers and healing skills, she used her extraordinary gifts to help, comfort and provide inspiration to many thousands of people from all walks of life. Her best-selling books have won her a legion of followers around the world, and few who have come into contact with her remain in any doubt at all that her gifts are both genuine and powerful.

Betty trained as a professional opera singer. She adored being on stage and loved to feel the pulsating energy of the audience. Betty never intended to become a healer but fate took a hand in her destiny and she became the very best.

Betty's first book, *Mind to Mind*, was published in 1989. Like Betty herself, it is cheerful, down-to-earth and full of humour. With a wide variety of case histories, it reveals how she became aware of her gifts and how she used her experiences of mind energy to help others. This was followed by *Mind Magic*, a *Sunday Times* Number One best-seller, which explains how mediums receive messages and evidence of survival, how absent healing is given, and how the Universal Mind links up with our intuition. And the third book in Betty's 'Mind' trilogy, *Mind Waves*, explores the energy which we all project and which invades everything around us, controlling not only our own lives but the world as a whole.

After a *Mind Workbook*, Betty went on to write her autobiography, *My Life as a Medium*, in which she describes her incredible personal journey into the world of healing and mediumship and the truly amazing encounters she experienced along the way. Three more books followed – *A Mind of Your Own*, which she dubbed her 'Book for Life'; *The Infinite Mind*, which examines the proof for the independence of the Mind from the physical Brain; and *A Free*

*Spirit*, which explores the relationships we all have with the planet, with animals, and with each other. Along with her three mini-books, *Clear Your Mind, Free Your Mind* and *A Little Book of Cosmic Colour*, Betty always tried to offer something different in each of her books, and the thousands of letters she would receive each month were the proof that she succeeded!

Betty had a marvellous ability to communicate and was funny and warm like a close friend. Through her books and tapes she will continue to be that friend to thousands of people all over the world. Betty's incredible books were written in a very simple, clear and truthful way, giving the reader a formidable insight into complex issues that most writers are too nervous to address. Her books contain true stories and observations that capture the imagination and make people think.

Betty reached out to everyone and touched their soul with her sense of humour and love, which only a truly magical spiritual teacher can do. She used her gifts and energy in a wonderful way to enable those she touched to develop a new and positive outlook on life. In fact, Betty helped so many people to overcome the fear of death that I can only imagine there were some joyful celebrations on the 'other side' when Betty made her transition from this world on 26 March 2002 – our loss their gain!

Betty's surname 'Shine' was very appropriate because she was so so radiant and full of light and energy that she could have lit up a power station! She always said, 'To give is better than to receive,' and she lived up to her philosophy. She bridged the great divide between this world and the next, and her soul will live on to begin the next amazing chapter of her life. Betty *is* a truly remarkable person.

Thank you, Betty, for your love and unbelievable spiritual guidance. We all know you will be with us forever.

JANET SHINE

# SHINE ON
## *Visions of Life*

# BETTY SHINE

HarperCollins*Publishers*

HarperCollins*Publishers*
77–85 Fulham Palace Road,
Hammersmith, London W6 8JB

www.**fire**and**water**.com

Published by HarperCollins*Publishers* 2003
1 3 5 7 9 8 6 4 2

ISBN 0 00 716081 X

Set in Bembo by
Rowland Phototypesetting Ltd, Bury St Edmunds, Suffolk

Printed and bound in Great Britain by
Clays Ltd, St Ives plc

To BETTY SHINE
in memory of a very special soul.

# Introduction

*Poetry is the spontaneous overflow of powerful feeling.*
*It takes its origin from emotion recollected in tranquillity.*

WILLIAM WORDSWORTH

1770–1850

This evening I have been compelled to sit at the computer and relay the story behind the poems and lyrics that you will read and absorb into your hearts.

In the last 18 months of her life, Betty spent night and day writing about situations that had touched her heart and soul. She was so moved by all that she heard, saw and read that she was able to put all these emotions down on scraps of paper, backs of envelopes, notepads – the ideas came thick and fast, sometimes so fast that she could hardly get pen to paper in time. She would often relay messages from the spirit world in her writings, understanding all that they had to say and putting it down as it was spoken to her. Automatic writing often occurred at any time of day or night – when messages are passed through from spirit you have to act upon them, even if you are in the bath! This she did, never denying a channel of thought from spirit to herself.

She always wrote from her heart. The most overwhelming time was during the September 11th tragedy. Without Betty realising it, she foresaw this tragedy happening. She had channelled automatic writings, even drawings of planes colliding in mid-air, smoke, bodies, in fact all the images that you would have seen on the television screen. Betty would say, 'These images I am getting are unbelievable.' Though none of us knew what it meant, she actually saw it all before it happened! That is how utterly amazing she was as a clairvoyant.

I would arrive at Betty's house in Sussex where she lived and worked, ready for my day's work ahead. Even before I could get in the front door she would say, 'Janet come into the living room – I've got another masterpiece to read to you. I wrote it last night.' I would stand with bated breath as I knew how her heart and soul had gone into these poems. As she read each piece of work to me, the tears would often well up in my eyes as they were so beautiful, funny, sad or true to everyday life that we all experience. 'What do you think?' she would ask. 'Fantastic,' was always my reply, because they truly were. Her eyes would light up and we would then put all these writings into a special folder knowing that one day someone somewhere would read them. It was always her dream to have them published or the lyrics recorded, as she truly believed that, like all her books, these special writings would move the hearts and souls of her public. I believe they will too, and that is why I was determined to have them shown to the world as a very last tribute to Betty's tremendous courage through a very difficult 18 months. These writings kept her determination and pure mental and physical strength going when all was against her, and without the hope of the afterlife Betty would have never coped with her physical ailments on earth. She fought to the bitter end and made me so proud of her.

I will never forget her grabbing my hand every day when I arrived for work, that warm, chunky, healing hand, so full of love and energy. She would not let go until she had told me all her news! Even now when I sit quietly I can feel that hand in mine. Betty was passionate about life on earth and life beyond, and I hope that by reading this book you will be able to share in the same passion that she had.

JANET SHINE
December 2002

# SHINE ON

# 1

## *Book of Life*

This poem really says it all. Betty's whole life was about communicating with people, spirits, plants and animals. She loved writing, and her ideas would flow like crystal-clear water. With pen to paper, she produced the most amazing work. Each page of every book is filled with wisdom, insight, hope and understanding, stemming from her own life's experiences. Her main goal was to bring simplicity to the subjects of healing, mediumship and spirituality, and this she achieved with great success – even hardened sceptics were convinced of a world beyond. Such was her nature, Betty gave of herself and her knowledge without want of anything in return. Throughout her life she stayed true to her beliefs, writing with no fear of ridicule, which often took tremendous courage. The titles and covers of every one of her books were most important to Betty as she felt that her energy would impart itself to those who held and read each book, which indeed it did to millions of readers. The books Betty wrote were 'the books of her life', and what a truly amazing life it was!

In the pages of my book,
You'll find mystery and love,
Emotions that are bared
And tragedies shared
It's all there.

It has taken a lifetime
To write all the words,
But what is a lifetime
If at last you are heard?

The giving and forgiving
Are the most important lines,
For when you get to the end
There's no time to pretend.

You'll find the characters inside
Weren't saints all the time,
But maybe you'll discover
Within the cover
Inspirational lines.

The book, it's not a work of art,
But the words inside
Describe chapters of my life
That taught me how to survive.

It has taken a lifetime
To write all the words
But what is a lifetime
If at last they are heard?

And I hope within the cover
You'll discover
Inspirational lines
That will teach you how to survive.

# 2

## *A Pot of Gold*

How many times have we told our children, 'At the end of the rainbow you will find a pot of gold'? This image captures the imagination and encourages us to strive for success. Many think that success is measured in material wealth, others think it is achieved by finding God, but Betty classed her pot of gold as knowledge in all things. The more knowledge we gain, the more understanding of life we have and the more we can help others.

Knowing ourselves is the first step. We all have two sides to our nature and sometimes that can be hard to face, but knowing this fact enables us to become more positive about ourselves and change if need be. A pot of gold is found only through pure hard work and determination, and for that you have to have courage.

I am a dreamer,
Who walks the corridors of light
That gives me life.

The mirrors that I see
Show other sides of me
And tell me who and what I am.

This truth is hard to take
But it brings a kind of ecstasy
In the knowledge that it brings.

We're told we must never go
'Where angels fear to tread'.
But in my dreams, I took that path
And found a pot of gold
That others hadn't dared to hold.

I had a choice, to take it in my hands
And walk away, or take a simple scroll
Which held the mysteries and the vibes
That the 'ancients' had withheld
And had guarded with their lives.

The choice was mine and mine alone.
I do not know what choice I made
For in an instant I was wide awake.

But I do not have material things
But a gift of 'knowing'
That I know cannot be bought or sold
For a pot of gold.

# 3

## *Our World*

There were so many poets that influenced Betty's life, and one special to her was W.H. Auden. He wrote poems and cabaret lyrics in the thirties including 'Funeral Blues' which was read in *Four Weddings and a Funeral*. He also wrote a libretto for the Benjamin Britten opera *Paul Bunyan*. He was a great scholar and always wrote about social issues, and Betty always felt an affinity toward him. Auden died in 1973, leaving three posthumous poems to be printed after his death. Betty did the same with the poems in this book – I am sure they both have much to talk about in the dimension beyond!

Will you accept
From the mind of a child
A simple concept
That people inept
Unable to fathom
How to regain
A world without pain
Should relinquish their tasks
To alleviate anguish
And fear of the past
That was nurtured by hate
So that we may restore –
Not kill and deface –
Our World?
This beautiful place.

# 4

# *Love At First Sight*

How many of us have experienced 'love at first sight?' When love touches a human soul it changes it forever. The instant attraction, the change of energy that cascades through us, it is truly an experience not to be missed. There seems to be instant recognition, rapport and waves of energy that pass between two people, a feeling of 'Oneness'. When it happens you are helpless, you lose all rational thinking, the 'love' takes over. Many believe that they connect emotionally with another person because perhaps they have known them in a previous life.

With 'love at first sight', we experience romance, something sometimes forgotten. One day it will happen to you.

Sparks, like stars blowing in the wind,
And a light that glows, as our emotions overflow,
Can only be the beginning,
And not the end.

There is no day, no night; this is love at first sight.
And as the earth moves beneath our feet,
And the world spins around, we hold on,
For we are but mortals walking on hallowed ground.

There is no care of who we are, or have been.
We have emerged, as though from sleep,
Like butterflies from a chrysalis.

In an instant we understand,
It is the lightning strike that is only given once
In any lifetime.

There is no day, no night, this is love at first sight,
There is no beginning, and can be no end,
For we are but mortals walking on hallowed ground,
And we walk as one.

# 5

## An Extraordinary Man

Betty dedicated this poem to Michael Bentine, who was a very dear friend to Betty for nearly 15 years. Michael came along to support her at her very first book launch in Surrey. They had so much in common – spirituality, a true zest for living, humour, laughter, and they also shared the interest of writing. Michael insisted on writing the foreword to Betty's first book, *Mind to Mind*, in which he mentioned the tremendous healing that Betty gave him and his family over the years. Betty would travel to his home to give his dear daughter Marylla healing, and he wrote, 'Betty brought our child something very precious: the gift of comfort and mental peace. For that alone I will never be able to thank her enough.'

Michael, like Betty, was never afraid to admit to believing in the afterlife and he and Betty would chat for hours on this topic. When Michael became ill he would travel to Betty's home in Sussex for healing. They would laugh, cry, exchange stories of the past and most of all support each other. Michael was indeed a very Extraordinary Man, and I know that he and Betty are now together in spirit.

An extraordinary man
Whose eyes betrayed his soul,
For deep within the fragments of his heart,
The losses took their toll.

Teacher, preacher, comic, clown,
He was all these things and more,
And as the artist couldn't hide
The feelings inside
A canvas would light up
With his very special touch
And capture in a frame
Why he was born to fame.

An extraordinary man,
Who dazzled with his wit,
And with a smile full of mirth
A candle would be lit
Inside all who heard.

His loss is great
But his special gifts remain,
And I know that he's survived
As he speaks still
Of those he left behind.

He talks of love, humanity and trust
And the essence all around,
That unites this world and souls
Within the Universe.

He's a teacher, a preacher, a comic, a clown,
For Michael you will always be
The sum total of your Mind—
An extraordinary man.

# 6

## *Picking Up the Pieces*

*'Our deeds determine us, as much as we determine our deeds.'*

GEORGE ELIOT
1819–1880

The hard fact about life is that at some time we all fall from a great height, and as we fall we break – mentally, physically and psychologically. Our egos whirl out of control and it is very hard to put ourselves back together again. We all need someone, somewhere, to help us literally pick up the pieces – the dented ego, the torn-apart heart, the out-of-control thoughts. The encouraging thing is that we humans *do* mend and learn from our mistakes.

I'm picking up the pieces
And starting all over again.
My life has been fractured far too long,
It simply can't go on.

I've left a trail of emptiness
That I can't hide behind.
It should never have been like this,
I must have been out of my mind.

There's been no belonging, no owning,
I thought I was being smart,
I can't believe how wrong I have been
Right from the start.

Half of my life has been wasted,
But the other half won't be
Because I'm picking up the pieces
And starting all over again.

# 7

# *Eternity*

During Betty's career as a medium, healer and clairvoyant she would speak to countless clients who visited her about their near-death experiences. They all spoke of being in a dark tunnel and being propelled through this tunnel out into a brilliant white light. They spoke of being bemused, not knowing where they were or what was happening to them. Suddenly all fear disappeared and eternity had been found. It was such a consistent story from wildly different people that Betty knew it must be true.

I couldn't understand
The place I was in.
There was no space
I couldn't breathe.

Then I was on my feet,
Strange thoughts crossed my mind.
The heavens laid bare
By a golden light
I had just reached.

I have no fears,
For, if this is eternity,
I can now sleep
As I have never slept before.
I have found the door
I have been looking for.

# 8

# *Music Is My Life*

Music was certainly a huge part of Betty's life. In her twenties she studied opera and performed in many different operatic roles, one being 'Queen of the Night' by Mozart. Her idol was the great Maria Callas, for Betty's voice was identical – crisp, clear, enchanting and mystical. Betty's choice of music went from opera right through to pop. She would often go to musicals in the West End and talk for hours afterwards about the performance and how much she had enjoyed the evening. Betty knew many celebrities in showbusiness and the stage was a familiar place for her to be. She would always support up-and-coming young artists new on the scene, as she knew how terribly hard it was to make it in the music business. Frank Sinatra was her favourite artist and I often heard her singing at the top of her voice, 'I Did It My Way'! And so she did!

Betty could command an audience in a split second with her smooth, silky, hypnotic voice. In an instant you felt relaxed and at peace. Betty's healing tapes have sold for over 20 years and continue to be a great success. The lyrics that Betty wrote are in the process of being recorded and published, and as the last verse of this poem says, 'Then one day, I heard the music playing. And I realised that it was mine'!

I've had music in my life
From the day that I was born,
Everyday in every way
I listened and I learned.

Jazz, the classics, rock and pop,
Always cast a spell,
And never failed to take me
Into a fantasy world

Then one day, I had a mind
To show the world what I could do
But I was taught a lesson I'll not forget,
And the secret of success.

I was told, that without hard work,
You can never be the best
So I played and played
Until I dropped. I couldn't stop.

Then one day, I heard music
Playing from a corner shop,
And I realised that it was mine
And that I'd made it to the top.

# 9

## *I*

We use the word 'I' roughly 200 times per day. It is used in almost every sentence. At least once a day we need to detach ourself from 'I' and become 'we'. Giving ourselves to others is to find ultimate joy.

If we could rid ourselves
of 'I' we would understand
the reason why we are here
at all. It is not to ask
all the time for obedience
and love, to make others
thought forms of our imagination
but to accept they must be free
to develop their own personality
to perhaps, just 'be'.

If we could rid ourselves of
'I' we would be releasing
ourselves, living our own lives
without fear and expectancy
of reward. Individuality and
freedom can be attained if we
could rid ourselves of 'I' and
in the giving find the ultimate
reason for living.

# 10

## *My Perfect Place*

Having insight into the world beyond provided Betty with one of her greatest comforts. Starting from a very early age she had glimpses throughout her life of this unbelievable dimension. She would describe walking through a cloud or haze to see what was on the other side. Colours were always vivid, the landscapes had a deep mystery about them. She called it her 'Perfect Place' where she could be peaceful and rest her mind. This was one of her routes of escape from the physical body, and in times of stress she would travel there. We all need our own 'Perfect Place'!

Skies of violet and blue
and silver streams
lined with gem-like stones of every hue.

A trail of gold from passing wings
which leaves a mist of dust
that for one second blots out
the cloak of mauve
that hovers over distant hills.

Close encounters with creatures
whose peaceful countenance
sums up the life they never had,
and fills me with pity and with shame
of their past suffering.

The familiar become very different
things, on close encounter.
And an arch of yellow, blue and green touches the spot
where all the rainbows end.

# 11

## *Romantic Interludes*

Love affairs are powerful and addictive. They entail attachment, intrigue, involvement, and spasmodic relationships. With a love affair you seem to be sitting on a knife's edge, waiting for the next time when you will see your lover. We cannot always be virtuous – clearly there are times when we feel trapped in a situation and all we want to do is escape. When having an affair we plan secret meetings and cover our tracks, creating excitement and anticipation, until one day we no longer have to hide, we are free, and the romantic interludes continue in the union of two people.

Out of sight, out of mind,
That's how it used to be,
But meeting you,
I'm addicted
To romantic interludes.

Chances are,
We may never have met,
That would have been bizarre,
Because our fate was set
In a myriad of stars.

Even the planets agree,
It was all meant to be,
They were in line from the start,
And on a dark night I can see
Where we are.

Out of sight, out of mind,
That's how it used to be,
But meeting you,
I'm addicted
To romantic interludes.

I have never mixed music and moonlight,
Scared of what it might do.
But now I'm with you,
I'm addicted
To romantic interludes.

# 12

## *That's OK*

The origin of 'OK' is American, 'O' being 'all' and 'K' being 'correct'. All Correct. In today's scientific society it is rarely accepted that it is OK not to have all the answers to life's mysteries. We would all like to tap into a reservoir of knowledge and understanding, but very often the answers are not there. I believe that we can try too hard to justify life's experiences instead of observing and remembering them and using them in a positive way some time later. So it's OK *not* to have the answers or the understanding – we learn as we live our life through.

There are many things we don't understand,
And that's OK.
If we knew everything from the time we were born
How boring our lives would be.

So we all learn as we go along,
And find the strength along the way
From the lessons that we learn,
And that's OK.

So many times I have not understood
Why it has to be this way,
But it's always been the same,
And it will never change.

We all learn as we go along,
And find the strength along the way
From the lessons that we learn,
And that's OK.

# 13

# *The Shadow and Piano*

This poem was written for Russ Conway. Betty never met Russ but when she heard of his passing into spirit she was devastated. His music always touched her heart, and she always said that Russ was part of his piano and the piano was part of him. When he played, his hands would glide across the keys as though they were silk, and the music would sing its own song. What a talent! He brought happiness to millions of listeners and was able to capture the magic of the moment. I am sure Betty has him still playing those ivory keys in the world beyond!

There's a shadow on the ivory keys,
And a whisper of a tune
Ripples through the room like a silent breeze.
The shadow and piano fuse together,
As though the shadow cannot part
With that priceless piece of art.

Whispers of that tune are an echo
Of the days when the shadow and piano played
And leave everyone in awe
As they sing a song of ecstasy,
Then sadness of a time
When they will never play again.

There's a mist within the room
Formed like a cloak around them both
All at once protecting and concealing
The magic of the moment
When the shadow plays the ivory keys.

The mist is now a silvery light
And guides the shadow from the room
As it looks back at its friend.
But the piano doesn't stay behind.
For over time it has been given life
And has decided that the time was right
For them to stay as one.

Now the piano has a lifeless ring
And will never play again,
But the tunes can still be heard
If you sit as quiet as a mouse
On the outside of the house.

# 14

## Common Sense

'Just use your common sense.' We have all said it – and had it said to us! No matter how clever you may think you are, your actions will automatically be dictated by common sense. Common sense buys us time, stops us acting upon a whim, and makes us think a little before jumping headlong into something that may be not quite right for us. It gives us peace of mind because we know we have given our action some forethought. Common sense is wisdom.

At the top of the page upon which Betty wrote this poem was a comment to a friend of hers. It said, *'Dear Les, I thought this would interest you. I actually thought about this poem while I was writing it!!!! There's hope for me yet!'*

It's easy to be wise after the event,
So the wisdom you brought
Was heaven sent.
You taught me many things,
But the greatest gift of all
Was common sense.

Simple as it seems
It's the best teacher that has ever been.
I travelled the world seeking success
But nothing great was ever achieved
Because the missing link
Was common sense

It gives us time to find happiness
And time to make amends,
But most of all, it fills the heart
With something we all seek,
The peace that comes
With common sense

We are always wise after the event
So the wisdom you taught
Was heaven sent,
And I am now content
But where would I be now
Without common sense!

# 15

## *My World*

*Man does not come*
*To know the world*
*By that which he extorts*
*From it*
*But rather by that*
*Which he adds to it himself.*

PAUL CLAUDEL
1868–1955

Betty's world was all consuming. Her talents with healing, mediumship, clairvoyance, survival evidence and being a good listener took
up literally all of her time – time she gave to others unselfishly. She
would answer numerous phone calls from patients in desperate need
of help, and no one was ever turned away. She would answer more
than a thousand letters per week from equally needy people, and
on top of all that would write her best-selling books. How did she
do it? With great difficulty! There were just not enough hours in
the day. The unbelievable events that happened in Betty's world of
spiritual work will never be forgotten, especially by her patients who
visited her for a span of over 17 years. Her readers will continue to
learn new abilities for themselves, for it was Betty's dream that each
one of us could become our own healer.

My hands touch the earth,
I look into the distance
No structure disturbs
The natural panoramic scenes,
I look up and watch
The swallows in flight
And the buzzard hovering
against the sky.

This is my world,
This is the way I want to live
In an environment
Where nature calls the tune
And humans adapt
To the song.

Where flowers re-seed themselves
And grow in erratic confusion
And trees lean with the prevailing wind
Which caresses the cheek.

Here in this place
I will remain
And spend the rest of my life
Observing
The nature of things.

# 16

# *A Spiritual Bystander*

The horrific news relayed by radio and scenes shown on television on September 11th 2001 were the forces behind this poem being written. Millions of people all over the world were simultaneously confronted with destruction, tragedy and huge loss of life. How could such a terrible event ever be justified? A question we are still asking ourselves today. We try to make sense of grief so that we may have a little peace of mind. Friends, neighbours, colleagues and strangers gathered together that fateful day seeking comfort and security. A little bit of each of our souls went out to all those who lost their lives and their loved ones in such a meaningless way.

Betty wrote on this poem, '*I think this piece is unique and so comforting for those who suffered loss.*'

I saw them
In the passing clouds
As they were whisked away
On that September day.

The light that shone upon them
Could only come from God,
The trailing light behind them
Showed where they had come from.

From darkness into light they came
To circumvent the heavens
Until they realised, like me,
They'd reached Eternity.

# 17

# *I Met a Ghost*

Ghosts *do* exist! But what are they? Simply, they are souls that have left the earthly body and moved into spirit to take on an etheric form, becoming energy beings who can appear and disappear at will. We on earth tend to think that these souls are a hallucination, an illusion, until one day we see one with our very own eyes! We often perceive ghosts as sinister, frightening or spooky, but they are merely our shadowy friends who only want to help and reassure us that there is a world beyond our own. The mind cannot die, only the physical body does, so our spirit friends continue to help us from above.

Those of us who are privileged to encounter a ghost first-hand usually have all their doubts answered. I came up with a saying for this: '*He who sees a ghost sees all that is.*'

I met a ghost
Not eerie like,
But a host
That I quite liked;
Not mean of thought
Just thought he ought
To keep me company:
And when he left
I was bereft
For someone kind
Is hard to find.

# 18

# *Time*

*'Next to grace, time is the most precious gift of God. Yet how much of both we waste. We say that time does many things. It teaches us many lessons, weans us from many follies, strengthens us in good resolves, and heals many wounds. And yet it does none of these things. Time does nothing. But time is the condition of all these things. Time is full of eternity. As we use it so shall we be. Every day has its opportunities, every hour its offer of grace.'*

HENRY. E. MANNING
1807–1892

Time is something Betty never wasted. She would be up at six in the morning and keep her day occupied until late at night. She never believed in having a lie-in! 'What a waste of precious time,' she would say. As children, my brother and I would be turned out of bed early in the morning for the start of a new day with all the exciting events ahead of us, and even now we both use our time wisely. This is a lesson many never learn.

Time moves on relentlessly,
It's the only thing we cannot touch,
It waits for no one,
It cares not if you have wasted it.
Your life is not a prime event
It has its own.

Where it goes
Has always been a mystery,
An unseen force
That never seems to sleep.

You can change the clocks,
'Put forward or put back'.
It makes no difference,
It doesn't care how long
It takes to reach a sunset
Or to hail a dawn.

# 19

## *España*

In 1975, Betty moved to Spain. Her own mother had died a year previously and the grief she felt was so intense that she wanted to escape from her past and start a new life in the sun. This we did as a family – even the dog and cat came, as there was no way she would leave them behind!

A beautiful villa was built up in the mountains overlooking a tiny village called Moriara. The views were spectacular: rolling mountainside, vineyards, donkeys, and the view of the bay in the distance. It was truly heaven. We all lived here for five years, integrating with the locals, learning the language and enjoying the sunshine. Here Betty began to realise her potential in writing and began her first book. Her surroundings gave her tremendous inspiration and the one sight that always remained in her mind was the spectacular sunset that we had from the villa.

Sadly, circumstances were such that we had to leave Spain and return to England. Saying goodbye to all that beauty was a very difficult thing to do – but the memories remained with Betty forever.

I may never pass this way again;
Never see the sparkle of the mountain streams,
Of the waterfalls that look like glass
Upon the surface of the rock.

Wild goats that graze upon
The more bare and arid land,
The buzzard as it swoops upon some rodent,
And the shepherd with his flock.

The sunrise as it appears on the horizon,
Balanced on the sea, and the sunset,
A burning ball of gold that disappears
Behind a mountain range in a blaze of glory.

For when the autumn moon returns,
I shall be gone,
Away from this wild mysterious land,
Away from these sunny shores
And all their beauty.

# Unknown Forces

A lightning flash can generate a hundred million volts of energy, enough to light up a whole town. As human beings, we delude ourselves that we have control of the world – far from it! The forces of nature have the real power. A flash flood can wipe out a city in hours, hurricane winds can destroy hundreds of buildings, and an earthquake will shake the very foundation of the land we live on. We should look again at who and what is in control of our existence.

Lightning flashed across the sky,
And the clouds, for one split second,
Became an accumulation
Of many coloured pillows.

The earth, parched and brown,
Glowed like a bed of coals
As though brought to life
By giant bellows.

Not a sound could be heard,
No animal, no bird,
No sign of any life at all,
As the flashes danced around.

A force far greater
Than any mortals could produce
Was wandering about the heavens,
Occasionally to touch the ground.

In moments such as these,
There is no doubt
That we on earth are, indeed,
Very small.

These signs, perhaps,
Are to remind us, that it is
Only by the Grace of God,
We exist at all.

# *Pages in a Travel Book*

The mere thought of being able to travel gives most of us a sense of freedom, being able to explore new countries and cultures. The excitement wells up in us when we look through travel brochures or guides trying to take in all the information given. We turn page after page until finally we make a decision; by this time the pages are crumpled, tatty and the corners turned back, but the ultimate goal has been achieved – travel is inevitable! From the azure waters of the Caribbean to the crisp champagne snow of Canada, we dream and plan.

The memories of travel remain with us forever. We feed them with a record of our adventures, hence the photo albums we compile when we return. Our minds, though, remember much more – the taste of oriental food, the sound of a strange language, the hospitality of those we meet, and the sights we see that overwhelm us. None of these can really be captured on film, and at least for now we are contented until the next great adventure!

Beneath a diamond-studded, starlit sky,
I feel your presence here.
We had so little time to make our dreams come true.
This haunts me still.

Turned-down corners, on pages
In the travel books,
Remind me of those we took
And those that 'might have been'.

Mountain-tops like crumbled, wedding cake,
And trickling streams, which mirrored clear blue skies
On the surface of a lake we made our own.
It was our favourite place.

The walks we took along a shore
Leaving footprints in the sand.
A captured memory
On the contours of the land.

Now our book of dreams lies closed.
Like an unfinished melody
When tears are shed
And you find there is no end.

Beneath a diamond-studded, starlit sky
I feel your presence here
And as it warms me; I forget that I'm alone
On this cold, but beautiful, wintry night.

# 22

# *A Shattered Piece of Glass*

Have you ever noticed how beautiful a broken piece of glass is? If you hold it up to the light, it will show you many patterns and hues; if left on the ground, it will remain dull and sharp.

This is how we reflect ourselves too. The art is to stay in the light – and not to cut ourselves and cause pain.

My life is like a shattered piece of glass,
Where you can see a piece of art,
Or, if you are near,
A sliver that can cut.

When I hold it to the light
It can reflect the sun
But when the light is low
It shows the dark side of the moon.

But there are hues of blue and green,
When it's held against the sea,
Which gives me hope,
Because it's the better side of me.

That shattered piece of glass
Will be with me for the rest of my life
To remind me of a piece of art
Or a sliver that can cut.

And I'll change the pictures
One by one, until I can see
More of the blues and greens
That are reflected in the sea.

# 23

# A Bit of Light Relief

In today's society, children grow up so fast that somehow their minds whizz around like a spinning top. They soak up information like a sponge, always wanting to know 'Why?' Oh, the strain it puts upon the poor parents! But somehow they find the answers and the faces of these tiny minds light up with surprise – or grimace with disbelief.

We are the teachers, a powerful position to be in, which is why we must strive to give children the chance to explore our minds.

Mainly they are curious,
Try to be mysterious
And sometimes they are serious
Which comes as no surprise
To those who give advice.

But children are complex
And easily vexed
When they cannot understand
And defiantly stand
Plying us with 'Why's.

So from one who knows,
Be on your toes,
'Cos they won't give in
And you can't win,
Especially if you lie.

So you'd better find the answers
To the 'Why's.

# 24

# Changing World

We introduce this poem of Betty's with another poem, written by her friend, Patricia Irvine.

*Tonight, I have something deep in my mind*
*At lunchtime, with Paula, I met Betty Shine.*
*When I realised who she was, I rose to say 'Thanks'*
*In mind matters she's simply the First in the ranks*

*Indeed I have much to be grateful for*
*She encouraged me to find my own inner core*
*Once a hard-and-fast sceptic, my thoughts black and white*
*She helped me discover the true meaning of light*

*Endlessly she struggles to show us the way*
*With her books and her tapes each selfless day.*
*But I think it is time to award her a rest*
*After all, what's the point of destroying the Best?*

*Instead of our 'taking' let us send her instead*
*Light, Love and Healing each night before bed!*
*So here is our task, friends, both yours and mine*
*Together, help Betty continue to SHINE!*

Clouds reflected in the
Silent pool, moving slowly
Across the surface, first white,
Then revealing dark green depths
With waving fronds of weed.

A swiftly passing shadow
Of a bird on the wing,
Patch of bright blue sky,
Silver fishes caught in a
Shaft of sunlight – feeding.

A silent frog sits on a
Patch of water-lilies
Watching the antics of
The may-flies, reeds rustle
In the breeze.

A tiny nest with moorhen chicks,
Two bright eyes of a vole,
Dark clouds replace the white,
No sunlight now – no silent pool,
It is raining.

# 25

## *Secrets*

A wonderful word, *secrets*. It conjures up a sense of mystery, disguise, undisclosed information. 'It's a secret' are words spoken by many.

Sometimes, though, secrets are shared all too freely. '*Un secret de Polichinelle*' is an open secret, not a secret at all. Polichinelle is the Punch of the old French puppet shows and his secrets are stage whispers told to all the audience.

My heart knows the secrets of my nights.
I can't hide my despair,
And I can't put my thoughts into words
Because there's no one there.

I try not to think about the past
Because I know I had the best,
But now I can't escape
The loneliness.

Don't pity me, I knew the score,
She told me everyday,
That if our love didn't last,
She would go away.

But I couldn't have foreseen
How one-sided it would be
Because the love we had – for me –
Is not a might-have-been.

My heart knows the secrets of my nights
I can't hide my pain,
But I know I couldn't go
Through this experience again.

# 26

# *There Are No Words*

Zelda Fitzgerald was born on 24th July 1900 and died aged 48. She was married to Scott Fitzgerald, the writer, poet and playboy. Zelda was drawn into the life of society, at that time known as the 'Flappers', which consisted of outlandish parties and being reckless and unconventional. Ladies would search for self expression through fashion, music and dancing, all requiring money on a free-flowing basis. Zelda once said 'Oh it is so nice to spend money'. But behind all this so-called freedom of expression lay a very sad and lonely woman.

Zelda turned her talents to painting. She would show her work in different galleries until one day there was a fire that badly damaged the family home, destroying her precious work. She then used the themes of gardening, painting and religion as her subjects of art, but these exhibited more and more tendencies toward disturbance, pain, anguish and fear. She eventually rested as a patient in the Highland Hospital in Asheville NC. Fire eventually engulfed her there. In her last letter to her mother, Zelda wrote:

> *I am still sewing a blouse in occupational therapy, I miss seeing the new patterns. The weather is bien-faisant, soft breezes, the sun shining long and warm, the January jasmine is in full flower. I think of you all the time and wish I were with you expanding spiritually in the first spring sunshine. With dearest love and true gratitude for your constant love and devotion.*

> ZELDA FITZGERALD *March 1948*

It was this very letter that Betty 'saw' in a vision, the contents of which she was unsure of until she started to research Zelda Fitzgerald and uncovered an elaborate story. Such were Betty's stunning and overwhelming powers as a medium. This poem flowed through Betty one rainy morning early in March 2002, and she believed it to be from Zelda Fitzgerald.

There are no words to describe
The misery, brought about by
Someone else's inhumanity.

The mind becomes a child-like thing
Hanging on to everything,
Never wanting to let go,
Lest the union shows
A little bit of sympathy.

There can be no remorse or regret,
For somewhere within a part of me
I never knew, was a need to find a love
That was not only true,
But held within its grasp
A special kind of grace and dignity.

Alas, this was not to be,
And that special part of me
Withered away, and was lost forever
Until I found this place.

There are some things
That are never meant to be,
And will never know,
Until we reach Eternity.

# 27

# *You*

*Go confidently*
*In the direction of your dreams.*
*Live the life you've imagined*
*As you simplify your life,*
*The laws of the universe*
*Will be simpler,*
*Solitude will not be solitude*
*Poverty will not be poverty*
*Nor weakness be weakness.*

HENRY DAVID THOREAU
1817–1862

'*You create your own destiny*' was another one of Betty's favourite sayings. But do we know, to start with, who we are? A complex question that none of us can answer truthfully. Until we have found a firm identity, we find it difficult to place ourselves in society. For instance, at any interview, contest or talent show the first question usually asked is, 'Who are you and what do you do?' The answers given are sometimes quite comical and show that the true answer to the question 'Who are you?' is 'I am me.'

I sit and look
Around the room
And wonder why it is
That I have surrounded
Myself with all these
Meaningless, possessions;
Cocktail glasses,
Coffee tables,
Bits of this and that,
All enclosed by four, brick walls,
A roof and anonymity,
When all I long for
Is a timber shack
Nestling in the foothills of
Some warm and pleasant land,
Nudity to free my body
From these tiresome clothes and
To feel my bare feet
Sinking in the dewy grass;
One day, perhaps,
Sometimes dreams come true,
If this one does,
The only necessary part
Is you.

# 28

## *Cast a Spell*

Spells. A word that immediately conjures up thoughts of witches and cauldrons. But this is the stuff of fiction. To be spellbound is to be enchanted, charmed or transfixed by someone's smile or look. It transports you to a magical place. As I learned from Betty,

'*Cast a spell on me and I will be yours forever.*'

You always turn me on,
Especially when I'm down,
I think you cast a spell on me,
When I'm around.

What is the spell you cast
That changes everything,
And makes me thank God
For the gifts you bring?

If you tell me your secret,
I'll turn us into one,
Then when we're together,
I can turn you on.

I think you cast a spell on me,
Whenever you're around,
So tell me your secret,
And let me turn you on.

# 29

## *Life May Change*

All of us go through life-changing experiences – divorce, death, the birth of a new baby, or simply reaching a better understanding of ourselves and our life on earth. We have to embrace those changes and not be frightened by them. Invariably we learn about an inner strength we never knew we had, which we can pass on to others through advice, help and support. By adapting to change, we learn to communicate the key to all human existence.

Never leave words unsaid, deeds undone or goals unachieved, or you will regret it. Have the courage to fulfil your life's ambitions, and don't wait until tomorrow – it may be too late!

Life may change, hope disappear,
But deep within us all
There's a reason we are here.
We can't give up in the rainy seasons,
For when the storms have passed
There's still just us
And we have to find a way
To make the sun shine every day
And hear the music in the wind.

Every moment of our lives
Is a very special gift,
We can't return it 'til it's time to go.
So we have to find a way
To make the sun shine every day,
We have to see the light
In every moment of our lives.

And we have to repair
The damage we have done
Not only to ourselves
But to everyone who cared
Throughout the years.

From today our lives will change
We can't simply say we'll try,
We can't just turn around
And say goodbye.
For our lives are a gift
That we can't return
Until it's time for us to go
And that's not yet.

# 30

# I Asked God

God, the Almighty, the Creator, the Supreme Being, Powers Above. Let the Light shine on us all.

We all have some kind of belief whatever it may be, but one thing is certain – there is some almighty power out in the universe that watches over us. Religious or not, to have no faith at all is to be deprived of essential spiritual nourishment.

I asked God,
I promised him, if I survived
The danger I was in
I would serve His cause.
But I forgot the words I used,
I lived in sin and I abused
All spiritual things.

When I died, He didn't mind
But looked at me with some surprise
When I asked Him to forgive.
He said, 'Don't fret my child,
I can wait awhile.
Young souls need to grow
And learn that "knowing"
Is all they need to know.
This takes many lifetimes,
So I know in time
You will understand not me,
But understand the man.'

# 31

# The Man I Never Knew

There is a driving force behind us all – we have spirit helpers by our side, guiding us through good and bad times. Betty had such a helper, whom she knew as 'the Guru', and she would call upon his help in times of stress. She would see his spirit form and could feel his unconditional love for her.

When someone is very ill their spirit helpers meet them in their semi-sleep state, showing them the world beyond. Betty would often talk of such visits, many from her own family, her mother, father, sister, brother, and of course 'the Guru'. He showed Betty the spirit world, with its vivid colours, undulating landscapes, waterfalls, and the intense energy that pervaded everything. Distances were not a restriction, and she would describe how she would 'fly', known as Astral Travel. When arriving for work Betty would talk to me of the amazing places she had seen and experiences she had had, and because of her deteriorating health she and I knew that she was being prepared to pass over on to the other side. It was an unspoken realisation between us both. This is what made the bond between Betty and me so unique, for I shared in her tremendous abilities and learnt and grew by them. What a privilege it has been to have such a special spiritual soul as my mother. I know she is with me every day.

It was only chance
That took me to those ancient hills,
And made me listen to a man
Who I couldn't see
But the message was for me.
And it set me free.

I knew I had a task
But rocks and rapids blocked my path
And the dark storms overhead
Raged, until I bowed my head
And hid the lightning in the sky
That lit the night I couldn't see.

I wanted to be free
But the price was much too high
And I knelt upon my knees
And asked for clemency
And although I listened for a voice
I couldn't hear a thing.

Then suddenly the skies were blue
And a man I'd never met
Was walking by my side
And stayed until the journey's end
Then he disappeared from view
The man I never knew.

Now my life is at an end
I've walked the rugged paths
And fought the raging storms
And now I hope that I'll meet again
The man I never knew
At my journey's end.

# 32

# *Woman*

'*What is truly indispensable for the conduct of life has been taught us by women – the small rules of courtesy, the actions that win us the warmth or deference of others; the words that assure us a welcome; the attitudes that must be varied to mesh with character or situation; all social strategy. It is listening to women that teaches us to speak to men.*'

R. DE GOURMONT 1858–1915

My interpretation of the word *woman* is:

Warm
Open-hearted
Manipulative
Appealing
Naughty!

A young sapling is
Frail and needs care
And attention before
The first blossom appears;
The first fruit must not be
Allowed to ripen for
Fear of inferior crops later,
The pruning must be gentle
So that the shape will be
Beautiful and not a stunted image
And when eventually the tree matures
It will bear on its branches the
Fruits for which we have
So long waited;
And they will be beautiful;
So it is also with a woman.

# 33

# A Waxing Moon

One of Betty's many friends was Debbie O'Gorman who works at a leading department store in Haywards Heath. Debbie would always look after Betty when she went shopping in the store and over a number of months we all became very good friends. This is Debbie's memory of Betty:

'I found myself looking forward to Betty's visit every Thursday – she would always come and say hello. On one occasion we talked about how we would both love to live in Spain and soak up all that lovely sun. One week she seemed to know I was a little down and worried about my husband and she started giving me advice, which I took.

'I remember one day boasting to a fellow worker that I knew Betty Shine when a customer overheard and said that she had saved her life when her husband left her. She said, "I wonder if Betty has any idea how many people she has helped and how many lives she has touched?"

'The events of September 11th were a traumatic time. I was deeply touched as my husband's company had lost many colleagues and we were all in shock. That evening we were e-mailed a list of survivors and those unaccounted for and we were devastated at the news. A few days later I saw Betty. She told me that she had had a vision prior to the event, in which she saw planes and bodies, though not the details. "Did you tell anyone?" I asked. "No," she said. "Who would have believed me?" I think she would have been surprised. Betty told me her saying for those lost was, "We are not gone, we are just in the next room," and my heart felt lighter. I knew she meant that there is another life after death.

'Betty would often touch my arm when we were talking. Even in winter her hands were so hot, and I always felt healed by her. Some weeks later Betty did not seem so well and was so frustrated. Her mind was still as sharp as a knife but her body wouldn't always

A waxing moon and failing light
Hides the scenic reality
Of a dark, cold, winter's night.

The brevity of the moon's phases
Describes brief moments, in our lives,
For beauty, in any scene is short-lived,
And does not see another day
If the watcher doesn't watch carefully,
And retain those little moments
That entice the beautiful things
To come our way again.

Things are heaven-sent
But not to be used without concern,
For the gifts they bring
You will have to earn.

---

allow her to do all the things she wanted. When she became very ill at the end of 2001 I didn't see her for weeks, though Janet would give me regular updates. When she recovered she looked so well, her eyes shining and her skin as clear as a baby's.

'The last time I ever saw Betty was just after her birthday on 8th March 2002. She was so happy having had a lovely birthday lunch. When my friend rang me and told me the news that Betty Shine had died, I was devastated. I loved her so much, she was such fun. I am so proud that I knew her.'

# 34

# *Perpetual Light*

Light symbolises everlasting life.

*'There is a light that shines*
*beyond all things on earth*
*beyond us all, beyond the heavens*
*beyond the very highest heavens*
*This is the light that shines in our hearts.'*
From the *Chandogya Upanishads*
(III, 13.7)

The candle is a symbol of everlasting life. In the song *Candle in the Wind* – one of Betty's favourites – the verse *'the candle burned out long before your legend ever did*, signifies Betty's everlasting light that shone and will continue to 'Shine On' for so many people.

There are no sunsets or sunrise
But a perpetual light.
Dark cannot exist in this
Very special place.

Voices whisper all around,
And a lake of liquid glass
Mirrors the shallows and the depths
Of my soul as I pass.

My time is short
Because the magic that surrounds
May erase the imperfections in my personality,
And I need them to survive
In this imperfect world of ours.

Do I grieve for those who don't believe?
No! From life to life we're given
Many special things,
But a glimpse of Paradise has to be earned.

And once having seen, no one can disfigure
The memories in any way,
Because they are immortal, and cannot live
In this very basic place.

In this world of ours there is no night,
And we sleep not like mortals do
But with a single thought that closes the mind,
Until another thought wakes us up,
And we find we're in Eternity.

These are very special words,
And in them you will find the secret
To an everlasting peace
And happiness.

# 35

# The Mirror in the Hall

A mirror is a polished surface of amalgam-coated glass which reflects an image – a looking-glass. Every time we look into a mirror we can see a reflection of ourselves, and not just the physical image, also the aura, the energy field around us. The aura can be seen in many different colours, reflecting how we are feeling or thinking at that particular time.

It has also been known for spirit people to show themselves through the mirror, making it easier for the recipient to see them. The next time you look into a mirror, remember anything could happen!

The mirror in the hall
Reflects your face,
You have left behind a part of you
I can't erase.

In the morning
I can see your smile,
But when the lights are low
I can see another side of you.

The loneliness, the pain,
Are etched upon your face,
And I know now
Why you couldn't stay.

All I have left are the memories
Some of shame
That's why I know
You won't be coming back again.

But the mirror in the hall
Reflects your face,
And that part of you
I don't want to erase.

# 36

# *Two Wrongs Don't Make a Right*

When we are confronted with a situation that deeply hurts us, we instinctively put up our defences and seek revenge. We become increasingly eager to set the records straight and make out that we were not the guilty party after all. It is so easy to want the upper hand, and through that desire look for ways of perhaps tricking the other party. Two wrongs certainly don't make a right! Our plans inevitably backfire on us, the tables are turned and our pride is hurt even more. We lose our dear friends, all respect has gone. The key that opens the door to justice and rehabilitation is *humility*. It is yours for the taking – embrace it with arms open wide, and your life will be an easier and happier one!

Two wrongs don't make a right.
I wish I'd known that from the start.
I found a love I thought would last
But it wasn't right.

And when I had the chance
To make amends,
I made the wrong choice again.

I wish I'd listened to my friends,
They were wiser by far
Than I had ever been.

There was something in my make-up
I couldn't understand.
And then when I understood
It was too late. I'd done it again!

Two wrongs don't make a right.
I wish I'd known that from the start,
When I finally understood
It was too late to make amends.
I'm sorry, my friends.

# 37

# *Footsteps in the Sand*

Imagine standing on an empty beach, the clear blue sea lapping against the golden sands. You begin to walk forward, and as you do so you can feel the sand parting beneath your feet; a footprint appears – yours – a signature that you existed on this beach for a while. A trail of prints is left as you walk into the distance, into a new time and place. The prints remain in the sand until the sea gently washes them away forever.

Footsteps in the sand,
Formed in the contour of the land,
Invite me to explore
What lies beyond
Where the footsteps trod.

Where did they begin?
Where do they end?
What will it mean
If they disappear from sight,
Is it a sign?

I need time to think,
But time's not on my side,
In this sun, sand and sea
Paradise.

As I look to the horizon
I can see the world outside
Waiting to claim me
As its own again.

The footsteps in the sand
Where did they begin?
Where do they end?

I need time to think
But time's not on my side
In this sun, sand and sea
Paradise.

And yet, the footsteps urge me on
To explore and leave behind
Forever,
The world outside.

# 38

# Lighten the Darkness

*Only a world that is*
*Truly human*
*Can be a world*
*That is peaceful and strong.*

POPE JOHN PAUL II
1920–

Peace is something we are all looking for at this time of global unrest. Betty found peace in listening to music and practising meditation. Five minutes of meditation was always recommended to all her clients, showing them that peace can always be found amid the turmoil in our lives.

Lighten the darkness
Of the hour
Lest we possess
Such power
That leaves shadows
We can't erase,
Can't move, or
Phase out thoughts
That men ought
Never give time to
Lest they hear evil
In their midst.

Losses wrought
With time bought
Make rivers flow
Red beneath
The moon's glow.
Heed the clarity
That binds the soul
That makes us whole.
Make this vow,
Look for peace now,
Do not seek
Exciting things,
Pay heed
And you will
Rest In Peace.

# 39

# *Promises*

How many times have you made a promise and broken it? All of us have done this at sometime, but what we don't realise is that a broken promise can cause a broken heart. Upon a promise we give our assurance that we will or will not do something. It usually indicates that there will be a good result, so expectation of achievement is put in our minds. If you ever have to break a promise, do it face-to-face with the person in question – it is the most courageous way.

Remember, if you make a promise, it is best to *keep it*.

We never said goodbye,
I didn't have the chance.
Promises you made
Were scattered in the wind
When our love came to an end.

How could you let this happen
When we shared so much?
I can still feel, through the magic
We shared, your tender touch.

A letter doesn't give me
All I need to know,
It is just an empty thing,
That flutters in the wind.

One day you will know
It's not the way to act,
For life has always proved
That what we do in life
Always comes back.

# 40

# *Forever in a Memory*

It has been recognised for centuries that music is a great healer. Sonic tones vibrate through every cell in the body, helping to keep the structure healthy. Music can affect us psychologically too, altering our conscious and unconscious mind. A song – comprising words and music – can have an amazing effect on us, so it is not surprising that we often associate a particular song or tune with times in our lives when perhaps we lost a loved one or we fell in love, and each time something is played our emotions soar. Words and music are powerful tools indeed.

Words and music –
Can there ever be
A greater healing
For humanity?
Poignant words and chords
Forever in a memory
That will remain
And will sustain
By just remembering.

# 41

# Listen to the Wind

Never allow the romance to die within a relationship. Transform the dullest of days into something warm and wonderful. The mind waves that flow are gentle and caressing – you will never be alone.

Betty was such a romantic, always wanting and seeking the perfect love affair and the perfect partner. Though this never materialised for her, she always had one true sweetheart – my father Leslie. Throughout their married life and even after, Leslie and Betty always had deep feelings for each other and remained the closest of friends, right up until Betty's passing. Bless them both.

Would that I could pluck a star from the sky
And pin it in your hair
Or bottle the heavy scent of flowers that pervades the
    atmosphere,
Capture the moon's glow in a crystal ball
Or seal my love into a phial
So that it may comfort you when you so desire.

Would that I could harness the wind
To blow you a kiss every night
Or coax the nightingales to sing at your window
When you put out the light,
Ask the spiders to spin a lacy gown like a second skin
Or maybe persuade the dewdrops to dance together
To form a pool for you to bathe in.

Would that I could give you these things
So that the memory of me would remain
Until I can be with you
And hold you close again.

# 42

## *Fear*

Fear (noun) *Unpleasant emotion caused by exposure to danger; expectation of pain, alarm, dread.* These are the dictionary definitions, but what really *is* 'fear'? All of us have at least one major fear that we carry around with us for most of our lives. Though we try to combat it, face up to it or suppress it, at the end of the day it always seems to remain in our conscious or subconscious mind. The way to tackle this is to turn it from a destructive force into a positive action or thought. Fear always stimulates the amount of adrenaline that we produce, so when we are confronted with a fearful situation and immediately want to run away, the adrenaline induces an energy rush and this in itself could one day save our life.

Fear also promotes the courage to go on when all is seemingly lost, another positive emotion. Musicians face the fear of the prospect of failing to perform well on stage, so their best abilities seem to surge through their minds and bodies for that given length of time, giving a brilliant performance. How often have you been frightened by another person? Your husband or wife, a colleague or teacher perhaps? These people can make us feel like prisoners, and we lose all logical thinking and control over our lives.

With what I call 'Fearless Fear', we no longer have to hide or be too afraid to say what we think; we are courageous enough to fight back and progress on our own. It is something that takes practice, but sure enough the benefits will show themselves. As President Franklin D. Roosevelt said, *'Let me assert my firm belief that the only thing we have to fear is fear itself.'*

You can't be a genius without the fear.
It takes us into heaven and hell
And opens up the channels
That give you inspiration.

Nothing can work as well if there's no need.
It's the terror inside
That opens your mind
To give you the masterpiece.

# 43

# *Miracles*

We often say 'Miracles can happen' without really believing it – but they truly can. As Betty's daughter and helper, I witnessed the most amazing miracles. Betty gave contact healing for over 20 years, 16 hours a day sometimes. Every client she saw for healing, clairvoyance or mediumship had an amazing experience: their hearts were lifted, their hopes soared, their mental and physical pain dissolved away.

In all the books that Betty wrote, she describes in detail miracles of love and healing, quite incredible accounts of what happened. We all have the capacity to make even a little miracle happen – go on, try it!

Miracles, can you make miracles?
Can you light a fire
When there's nothing there?
Can you look deep down
Into my despair
And make a miracle?

# 44

# The Actor

Betty had many friends but one very special, dear friend was and is Ken Kennedy. Betty and Ken would chat for hours on the phone. Both had a background of formal theatre training and understood the hardships that you had to go through to succeed in showbusiness. Ken wrote:

'*My dearest friend Betty Shine wrote this poem especially for me because she knew how much I loved being an actor on the professional stage. Unfortunately this phase of my life didn't continue and Betty knew the frustration and sadness that it caused me. This poem sums up exactly my feelings when I appeared on stage.*'

I slip out of my skin
When I want to escape
From the prison that I'm in.

I can sing and dance
And recite poetry.
I'm the star that shines in the dark.

There's no doubt in my mind
That when I find me
I can do everything with ease.

I can walk through the town
In a state of Grace
And people will look as I pass.

And when I stand on a chair
And act out my lines
People will stare and applaud.

But only I know
How the tears will flow
When it's time for me to go

And live out the farce
That is my life
And into my skin again.

Weeks will go by
When I'll have to pretend
That I like normality.

Until I get the urge to search for me
And with arms outstretched
Go and stand in the limelight again.

# 45

# *I Am Coming Up Again*

To be successful in life – whether it be in our career, marriage, friendships or parenting – is to say the least challenging. However hard we try, there are always pitfalls along the way. The key is to stand our ground and have the strength to carry on, to have a new outlook on life and not be suspended in the past.

Walk along a more positive path of life and don't look back. As Betty wrote, '*I never have expectations of life, only dreams.*'

I may be down
But I'm coming up again.
I'm going to make my stand
And stake my claim to fame again.

I know I've only myself to blame,
For the life I lost.
But I have my dreams
And I want them back again.

# 46

# *Joy of Living*

*In a higher world it is otherwise;*
*But here below to live is to change*
*And to be perfect is to have*
*Changed often.*

JOHN HENRY NEWMAN
1801–1890

My motto in life is to enjoy every moment – tomorrow will take care of itself. So often our senses are clouded by bitterness, hate, greed and our own egos, but with these put aside, we can enjoy others' achievements and we can shape our own lives towards a more positive future.

Do we not owe it to ourselves
To take the love that others
Have to offer? To live with
Old ideas and habits is like
Swimming against the tide,
Tiring and useless. Eventually
We must give in or forever
Flounder desperately and
Forlornly in our own misery.

Do we not owe it to ourselves
To take the happiness we so
Badly need to make our lives
Complete? Every living thing
Needs to be nurtured with
Loving care to achieve the
Ultimate joy of living. And
Once having known, we should
Never settle for second best.

# 47

# Dancing Girl

Dancing was one of Betty's favourite pastimes. It was fun and kept her fit – when she was younger she had only a 19 inch waist! Young men loved her, for she was so light on her feet and graceful too. Music and movement always fascinated her – ballet, jazz, flamenco and ballroom were her favourite forms of dance. The discipline of dancers and the sheer strength and stamina dancers need to sustain a routine never failed to amaze Betty. When dancers perform, they glow with life force.

Dancing girl,
Is there ever a night
When you're not out there
Dancing?

Have you ever thought
There's another life
In the daylight you've never seen,
When you're dancing?

Who'd have thought
You'd live the kind of life
That brings people to their knees
When they're dancing?

And yet there you are
Reaching out
To claim the stardom
You think you've earned.

And while you twist and turn
There's only one thing
On your mind
And that's dancing.

You don't give a damn
You might be missing out
On a life you've never seen,
Because you're always reaching out
When you're dancing.

# 48

## *Make Peace Happen*

The world today is a very vulnerable place. Nuclear weapons, immi-
nence of war, famine, world disease, poverty – we still have no
answers to these situations. Why? One word. Greed. We have still
to learn to share, listen, improve or adapt, rather than each nation
wanting it their own way. What we don't realise is that time is
running out. We are all mortal, and in an instant we will no longer
exist on earth, where we could have made a difference. If each one
of us makes just one change to the lives of the suffering then our
existence will not have been in vain.

Don't leave it too late,
To make peace happen,
All around the world,
There's so much hate.

We weren't born for this,
Let's love one another,
So let's embrace it
Before it's too late.

There's so little time,
To make things happen,
And only so much hate
That people can take.

Each one of us,
Can make peace happen,
If we care enough,
And don't leave it too late.

# 49

# *My Secret*

*Love seeks one thing only: the good of the one loved. It leaves all the other secondary effects to take care of themselves. Love, therefore, is its own reward.*

THOMAS MERTON 1915–1968

We all have a deep dark secret that we seem to keep for ever. Children very often have a little box of secret things and say '*It's a secret*' when they play. Secrets are usually more trivial than we think and usually better shared – but do you have the courage to speak out about them?

My heart knows in silence
the secret of the days
and nights; I put into
words that which I have
always known in thought,
and my fingers touch the
naked body of my dreams;
nothing on this earth
can quench the fire within;
and though others more
wise than I tell me that
I sin, I know my spirit
must be free and I must
love the one, who in his
turn loves me; for without
love I am lost; and forever in a
void would be.

# 50

# *Yesterday*

The song 'Yesterday' by the Beatles was one of Betty's favourite lyrics. Betty said, 'What happens to us today shapes us as individuals for tomorrow'. This is so true! We always hold on to the past – this is where we came from and influences what we do now. We make our mistakes yesterday and learn to correct them today.

We are all part of yesterday
And some things never die,
Like the friends we had
When we were young
And the important things
We left undone.

The lies we told to impress,
And the constant dreams of success,
If only we had realised
When we had the chance
We let it pass, so easily,
Out of our grasp.

We are all part of yesterday
And some things never die
Like the friends we had
When we were young
And the important things
We left undone.

If we don't let the past
Into our lives
We'll never get it right
How else can we learn
Where it all went wrong
And how to get it right.

No matter how much we wish
We could leave the past behind
We are all part of yesterday
And it made us what we are today.
And I'd like to thank those we left behind
Who shaped our lives at the time.

Now we can only wait and see
What tomorrow will bring
But there's one thing, I know
We can't give in
Or we'll destroy the good things
That happened yesterday.

# 51

## *Familiar Faces*

We all have times in our lives when we lose a loved one to illness or old age. It is so difficult to come to terms with a loss unless we have people who are close to us, supporting us through these testing times, familiar faces who give us strength and love, helping us to understand what has happened. No words need be spoken when we have these exceptional people around us.

One by one I have lost
the people most dear to me,
familiar faces, all have
disappeared. I took
for granted all the things
that mattered then suddenly
I looked around and found
I'd lost them all.

So hold me close, don't
ever say goodbye, because
without your love my life
would have no reason. Your
smiling face is with me all
the time and without your
love the years would have
no seasons.

Familiar faces, all have
disappeared. I took for
granted all the things
that mattered, so do not
leave me, please don't say
goodbye, for my life is just
beginning and you're the
reason why.

# 52

# *A Gift*

A statue is a representation of everlasting life. A beautifully sculptured image of all that was and could be. The human form has always been the most admired form of sculpture, a form of art requiring precision, eye for detail and the use of organic materials, and through the centuries we have seen it depicted in all its intricacy.

A dear friend of the family, Ken Kennedy, has given us a gift of a beautiful marble statue of a serene young lady with everlasting youth, set uon her own pedestal. A gift of love that was actually chosen by Betty for her garden 18 months before she died, I have put it in my own courtyard garden among all the plants that Betty kept to be seen by whoever visits. Now I feel her close to me, as I know the presence of Betty's spirit lives on in this statue.

It was here in the square I first saw her,
Standing there, quite bare,
With rounding bottom and sloping shoulders,
And beautiful long straight hair.

Her legs were long and delightful,
Slim fingers and long slender hands,
Lovely breasts and neat little navel,
A gift for any man.

Her lips were a perfect bow,
Eyes a very light grey,
But alas! she was made of stone,
And her pedestal of clay.

# 53

## *It's Freedom I Seek*

Inner strength is the key to freedom of mind and body. Each of us will find a shining light within that will give us hope, strength and peace. With these we can achieve anything without fear of ridicule. Human nature is such that we feel threatened when we come across people who are strong. We have to deal with these emotions and should take note of the other person's attributes. By adopting these qualities for ourselves we can create new opportunities that will allow us to proceed on to the next level of progression. So we can *learn* to be strong – what an exciting thought!

In the dazzling world
Of music and moonlight
I'm not bedazzled at all.
I have my own limelight
And only want to recall
The moments of laughter,
Of love and romance,
Of a life ever after
Not left to chance.

My world doesn't depend
On music and moonlight,
Or nights that are spent
On putting things right.
I need to be free
To have time to relax
And the freedom I seek
To not hold me back.

In the dazzling world
Of music and moonlight
I'm not bedazzled at all.
I've got my own light
And I can still recall,
When I found laughter,
Love and romance,
And a life ever after
Not left to chance.

Freedom comes at a price,
People come and they go,
But I'm sure I will find
A safe place to sow
All the seeds of life,
And Time . . .
To watch them grow.

# 54

# *Don't Make Me Cry Again*

The Bible says, '*O hear my cry O Lord.*' When we cry, we are appealing from within ourselves for some kind of release from pain or mental turmoil. Crying is the most therapeutic thing you can do – it cleanses the soul and heals the mind. Once we have released that tension and negative energy, we seem to feel lighter and more centred. We perceive life to be a challenge and move forward with new energy and determination.

> '*She would have made a splendid wife,*
> *for crying only made her eyes more bright.*'
> O. HENRY
> 1862–1910

Don't make me cry again,
Shed my tears in vain,
It's a waste of life
If you're not coming home.

Prints upon the windowpane
Show how I wait in vain
Just to hear your key
Turning in the door.

Don't make me cry again,
Shed my tears in vain,
It's a waste of life
If you're not coming home.

I feel a lightness in my step,
I'm walking back to happiness,
I'm taking back my life
So I can start anew.

I'll never cry again
Against the windowpane,
Shed my tears in vain
If you're not coming home.
The pieces of my heart
That you tore apart
I'm taking too.

# 55

# A Shadow of Myself

Ageing is a process none of us really wants to face up to – we cannot escape it however hard we try. With age come many illnesses, one being loss of memory, which can be a very painful process as slowly we find it harder to remember who people are, their names, or what we did when we were younger. Frustration sets in and suddenly we want all the answers at once. We can only hope that if it happens to us there will be someone with us who knows us well and can help us with those answers.

I'm a shadow of myself
Who always loved to dance
And discuss basic things,
The fabric of my dreams
And my great romance.

Who is it, looking back at me
From the mirror on the wall?
I don't recognise the face,
Why is she staring into space?
Can someone tell me?

Words in my mind
Have no reason or rhyme,
I think they might suggest
A certain happiness
From another time.

Who is it, looking back at me
From the mirror on the wall?
I don't recognise the face,
Why is she staring into space?
Can someone tell me?

Out there, somewhere,
Someone's waiting for me.
But first of all, I have to recall
Who I used to be,
That other side of me.

That's why I want to know
Who is looking back at me?
I don't recognise the face,
Why is she staring into space?
Can someone tell me?

# 56

# *The Same Night Sky*

How lovely it is to stand on a crisp clear night and gaze up at the stars which define each constellation. Some believe the stars show us our future, our destiny – we can only wait and see.

In the northern hemisphere, in countries such as Norway, Sweden, Canada and Scotland, you can sometimes see a shimmering curtain of light, huge glowing patches in the night sky. The name commonly associated with this is the 'Northern Lights' or the 'Aurora'. These lights have been seen for millions of years – yellows, blues, greens, reds, the colours twist and turn forming patterns; some look like curtains blowing in the wind. If you get the chance, it is wonderful to witness such a phenomenon.

Are we sharing the same night sky
And looking at the stars
As we used to do
So many moons ago?

Or are we so far apart
That your day is my night?
Have you found someone new
Who has captured your heart?
I wish I knew.

There's no star in the sky
That shines brighter than you used to.
You were my light in the dark
But we have drifted apart
And I have to know.

Are we sharing the same night sky
Or is your day my night?
Have you found someone new?
I wish I knew.

# 57

# Let Me Light Up Your Life

It's the responsibility of all parents to give their children as much encouragement and positive thought as possible. I know it is hard, especially when the child is moaning and groaning, but that, is when the encouragement is needed the most. Exam time (what hell that can be for us all!), breaking up with the first boyfriend or girlfriend and not having self worth – these situations require patience and words of wisdom. Betty's poem sums up the message of hope to all those who are struggling against a very tough world out there.

Let me light up your life,
Let me show you the way
To live every day.

Life's too precious to waste,
You can't keep hanging around
With nothing in mind.

You need to reach for the heights,
And forget the lows,
Find inspiration inside
To make you glow.

There's no reason or rhyme
You can't be the best
Because you have what it takes
To beat the rest.

Let me light up your life,
Let me show you the way
To live every day.

Just stop messing around
And playing the clown,
Then you'll find what you need
To succeed.

# 58

# Men and Machines

As I was writing this I heard the terrible news of the bomb attack at a nightclub in Bali. Scenes of bodies and metal flying everywhere; hundreds lost in the fire and flames of destruction; souls flying to heaven before their time; loved ones seeking knowledge in the hope that they might find a person who is missing. Stillness follows utter turmoil, heads lowered and hearts broken. How can this kind of destruction continue? We must find a way to stop terrorism before it destroys us.

Where men and machines
Line up together
I wonder whether
We know who we are?
Flesh and blood against metal and guns,
No one can win, it's a sin.
Look closer still
In the eyes of a child
Who has only known ill
When all the while
People degrade.
They enjoy the self-made
And the sickening sight
Of all who parade in the limelight
With jewels covering up
The idiocy of thought
In all those who see
And think 'that's for me!'
While children die, starvation abounds,
While the serpent of death slithers and slides
And hides . . . till it strikes
With all of its might,
While the world fetes the stars
And cannot see they're not gold
But worthless beneath,
Outwardly beaming,
Empty shells who do not think
Of the children who cry
And the children who die
Whilst they feast.

# 59

# *It's Not Over 'til it's Over*

Betty loved this poem as it reflected how she would deal with people and situations. She never gave up on anything or anyone – she would see the positive side to a situation and go with it. By talking through with her clients their worries and problems, she would make them see there is always an answer.

It's not over 'til it's over,
Don't complain, but just explain
What has changed so much, so quickly,
That you feel you have to leave.

Close the door for just one moment,
Put the cases in the hall,
Just let's hold each other close
And sit down and talk it through.

The good times, the bad times,
The love we shared.
The tears, the laughter
And how much we cared.

We can sit and talk
The whole night through.
For as I look at you, I know,
It's not over 'til it's over.

# 60

# *Where Is My Life?*

Time passes us by so quickly. We always think we have enough time to accomplish all those dreams we have, so we leave them until another time. But slowly time catches up with us. Daily events take over and our dreams are not realised.

It's an old adage, but never has a truer word been said – *'Never leave what you can do today until tomorrow.'*

Where is my life?
Where has it gone?
I want to know
Where I went wrong.

I turned my head, and then
When I looked back again
It had disappeared.
How did it happen?

Time was of no essence
I thought I knew the score
I could use it, or waste it, it was my time.
But it isn't any more.

Where is my life?
Where has it gone?
I want to know
Where I went wrong.

There must be something
I can do,
It can't just disappear from view.
This can't be the end.

Where is my life?
Where has it gone?
I want to know exactly
What went wrong.

Then I can use everything I've got
To put it right again.
And I won't waste it
Any more.

# 61

# We Are Together

Together but alone *or* together as one? How often have you been in someone's company but felt that they are miles away in their own thoughts, not connecting with you at all? It is easy for us to switch off when in the company of those who bore us, but this reaction can become a habit and we must remember that everyone has something valuable to offer.

We are together
And yet I am alone;
We smile
But my thoughts are my own;
We speak
But the words have no meaning
For that which is missing
Is love.

We are together;
We smile
And my thoughts are yours also;
We speak
Although words are not necessary;
For that which we have
Is love.

## 62

# *Heartbreak*

This sad poem was written for a close friend of Betty's who lost his wife in a terrible fire. He turned to drink to console and suppress his grief, but no amount of alcohol could drown his sorrow. One day his wife appeared to Betty from spirit and gave her a message for her husband. From that day on, Betty's friend never questioned the afterlife, but he moved forward with his life knowing that his wife was safe in spirit. He became a successful local playwright and coined a motto for himself. '*Memorise happy times centred in joy.*'

From day to day
I was writing essays
Alone in an empty room,
When from out of the blue
Came the news that my wife
Had lost her life in a fire.

What a waste, what a crime,
That someone so fine
Should have ended like this.
Her life hadn't been bliss
But she'd known happiness
In the past.

Now I live with the pain
Of long-lost refrains
And the face of an angel I knew so well
Who tugged at my heart
When we were apart
And yet together life was hell.

From that moment in time
I went into decline
As the ghosts of the past seared my heart.
But it wasn't all bad,
So let's drink to that,
Again, again, and again.

# 63

# *Shadows*

We all have a physical and an etheric body. The physical body feels pain, sorrow and grief, whereas the etheric body does not, it only rests in pure peace. We have the ability to open our spiritual eye, sometimes known as the third eye, and we can then see beyond physical matter. Whenever you are dreaming, meditating or thinking deeply, you are drifting into a special ether that cradles you and protects you while you discover this new dimension.

I look for shadows
Hoping I will see
The outline of your face
And the way you looked at me.

I look for shadows
For they remind me of the past,
As we watched them change the landscape
Like an artist with a brush.

Living with the memories
And the way it used to be
They are my friends and remind me
Of a love I know can never end.

One day, when I can live without the past,
They'll disappear from view
And I'll stop looking for the shadow
That might be you.

# 64

## *Midnight*

Midnight. A time of mystery, reflection and moonlight. A time to think, to make plans, to hear the peace.

You have probably heard of the 'Midnight Sun' where the sun never sets. Close to the north and south poles, these areas where the sun stays up for weeks in the middle of summer are quite spectacular. The sun dips toward the horizon but never falls below it. People in the North Americas, Scandinavia and former USSR who live inside the Arctic Circle have learnt to adapt to perpetually dark winters and almost continuous summer sunshine. So next time you look up at the stars at midnight, remember elsewhere the sun may still be shining.

It was midnight, our time,
The only time we were alone;
You sat at midnight
And thought of everything you'd done.

I told you they didn't matter,
But the misery they brought to you,
Made me unhappy too.

Midnight was our time
You should have known I'd understand,
But when I held you, you had gone,
Into a life that was your own.

It could have been so good,
I understood,
But the guilt within your heart
Told me we should part.

Midnight was our time,
The only time we were alone.
And now you're on your own
It's midnight.

# 65

## *We Can Never Give Up*

'*Genius is one per cent inspiration and ninety-nine per cent perspiration*'
THOMAS ALVA EDISON
1847–1931

Giving up was something Betty never did. From trying to get her
first book published to striving to have her lyrics put to music and
have them recorded, Betty fought back through much adversity.
We owe it to ourselves to strive for what we believe in and aim for
what we want out of life – and never let anything get us down.

You can't be a genius without the fear.
It takes us into Heaven and Hell
And opens up the channels
That give you inspiration.

Nothing can work as well
If there's no need.
It's the terror inside
That opens your mind
To give you the masterpiece.

The artist, singer, composer, poet and all
Have to look into the level that's beyond comprehension
For inspiration from collective memories
to inspire us all,
And to put their art to the test.
No matter how it makes us look.
It really doesn't matter.

There are many styles we use to amuse.
But it has to be your own
Or you will be on your own.

# 66

# *When You See*

*Let knowledge grow from more to more*
*But more of reverence in us dwell*
*That mind and soul, according well,*
*May make one music as before.*

ALFRED LORD TENNYSON
1809–1892

We all have the ability to see beyond this dimension using the centre of intuition, the 'third eye' positioned in the centre of the forehead. When meditating, focus your awareness on this area as though you are looking into a clear pool of water. Colours will appear, forms even, and observe them for they will help you obtain clairvoyance – 'clear vision'. We all have the gift; if only we were to practise once a day for five minutes, that's all it would take to develop it.

When you see
Do not believe
But be aware
The eye deceives,
Feel the pain
Love, longing, hate,
For the soul
Decides our fate.
Oh! foolish friends
Do not pretend
Or trust the eye,
Only on the soul rely;
Let not the gremlins
Steal your friends,
Listen to your heart instead.

# 67

# *Hard Luck*

Circumstances of life cause us to feel hard done by, down on our luck. We always seem to think that the grass is greener on the other side. So often it is not. We must be contented with our lot, not always looking for more. Beauty can be found in the tiniest grain of sand and wealth in the loving touch of someone who cares.

Once in a lifetime something happens
To make your dreams come true.
It's never happened to me.

Some people have it easy
They just can't seem to lose,
And aristocrats born with silver spoons live on booze.
Why can't it happen to me?

What does it take to get a break?
Why do I get the bread and not the cake?
Why don't I ever get a cherry in a cherry cake?
I don't know.

Why do all the bills come to me?
When there's four in the family?
And why is selling wares on a market stall okay,
Until it rains?

I have no cover and no umbrella
And overhead the drainpipe runs down my neck.
What a pig my life is,
Why wasn't I born a king?
Then I could have everything.

But it couldn't happen,
It never happens.
It'll never ever happen to me.

# 68

# I'm On the Outside Looking In

We all deserve to be given a second chance when things go wrong in our lives. The stupid mistakes we make, the thoughtlessness, the foolish things we say – these can be put aside and forgiven. Put your trust in that person just one more time.

I'm on the outside looking in
Through the window in the hall,
I can see her tear-stained face
As she leans against the wall.

I'm on the outside looking in,
I thought we'd played our final chord,
But as the melody lingers on
I know that I'm the fool.

I've taken chances, played the field,
With no thought
Of those who trusted me.
Life's stupid games, that's all.

I turn the key and step inside,
I touch her smiling face
And as I feel her warmth, I know
I don't want to feel the cold
On the outside looking in.

# 69

# *Thoughts*

In her book *A Free Spirit*, Betty's relentless campaign against cruelty, both in the animal kingdom and our own, was very evident. The 'circle of stupidities', as she called it, is never ending. Betty was expert at communicating with all life-forms and she was able to interact with the environment, always striving to understand the smallest act of nature. She wrote:

  *'The pity is that we are all so insignificant in the scheme of things, and in the final analysis Universal Law will be the judge. All I can do to the best of my ability is to help the world to help itself'.*

I have walked a million miles
And seen a million things
That have disturbed my inner being.

The ecology of the Earth disrupted–
A vicious circle of stupidities
And man's inhumanity to man.

All natural instincts crushed by *en masse* education,
The tenderness of youth
Destroyed by facts and figures.

Where pernicious influences of the outside world
Had not yet reached,
Only there did I find peace.

And when the Earth has finally turned to dust
Will we realise that we have killed
The only source from which we feed.

# 70

# Another Time, Another Place

How often do we find ourselves in a situation where we love another but through no fault of our own they are not free? It takes courage to let that loved one go. To allow them to have happiness and fulfilment in their lives, not to destroy the life that they have built and strived for. It is possible to have many loves in our lives, but there is always one that is extra special.

Another time, another place,
You could have been a part of me,
I would have taken you by the hand
And explored another path
With you beside me.

But I've leaned against the wind
And lost too many times,
To take the chance, to win your heart,
And take you back with me.

I'd like to hold you close,
But I'd never let you go,
You have touched my heart
That's why we have to part.
Walk away and don't look back,
Find the love I never had,
And live your life for me.

Another time, another place,
We could have had it all,
But it was never meant to be,
So turn around, and walk away,
And live your life for me.

# 71

# *Possessions*

As time goes by we accumulate more and more possessions, surrounding ourselves with objects large and small. The house becomes cluttered and we lose the sense of space which once surrounded us. More than material objects, we actually need freedom to move. The simple life will give you far more peace and harmony. A life based on always wanting to have something new is less free than a life based on *doing*, *being* and *giving*.

Possessions are material
things that give but a
moment's pleasure – and if
by material things our
success is measured then
we are a poor return for
the life we have been given,
for 'tis a very precious
gift to be used for universal
matters. In the end we must
atone and will be judged for
ourselves alone, and not by
what or whom we own.

# 72

# *Understanding*

It is said to understand others you must first understand yourself. But how can we have experienced all the emotions? It takes a lifetime to do this, so what we can do is listen and guide our friends and family through the experiences we have already had. Understanding others requires tremendous patience and time, which sadly many people do not seem to have. We owe it to ourselves to develop these attributes, as one day we too will need understanding from others.

Across the lake
the mist rises and
swirls as the
rising sun warms
the atmosphere;
leaves drip with
dew, and as the
morning chorus
heralds another
day I feel your
presence here;
between us no need
for explanation
or excuse for each
other we have a
natural need,
and in the morning
close to nature I
feel the pressure
of your hand and know
forever we will be
as one, and you will
always understand.

# 73

# *Alone in the Dark*

'*The knowledge that you will eventually stand in the light will inspire you to bury the past and go on to new pastures.*'

BETTY SHINE
1929–2002

Alone in the dark,
I can still feel your hand on my shoulder.
You didn't have to leave,
We could have worked it out.

Through the night,
When I touch the pillow next to me
It's now an empty space
Where your face used to be.

When I close my eyes,
I can still feel you by my side,
I want to last the night
Because I always lose you
In the morning light.

Alone in the dark
I can still feel you by my side.
You didn't have to leave,
We could have worked it out.
But now I'm alone,
And the lights are out.

# 74

# Shades of Life

*God writes the gospel*
*Not in the Bible alone*
*But on trees and flowers*
*And clouds and stars*

MARTIN LUTHER
1483–1546

Life is full of colour – colours of different shades, whether the changing colour of the seasons, the colour of someone's skin, or the emotional highs and lows that we experience. Betty called them 'Cosmic Colours'. We can be influenced dramatically by changing light, and some people suffer from the deprivation of light causing seasonal depression. Surround yourself with the yellows that will brighten your enthusiasm, the reds for energy, the greens for your love life, and the purples for intellect. Look to nature to inspire you even more.

At this moment in my life
The grey skies have a tinge of blue,
The grass is greener than before,
The flowers
have a brighter hue.
Problems do not overwhelm,
The loneliness has passed,
For since I met you long ago
The shades of life are deeper,
And you, my friend, my keeper.

# 75

# *Pain*

*Your pain*
*Is the breaking*
*Of the shell*
*That encloses*
*Your understanding*

KAHLIL GIBRAN
1883–1931

This poem was written at a time when Betty was in great distress. Her health was failing, and her life flashed before her in many different ways. She would have dreams of her past and visitations from her departed family, and she suffered much pain and discomfort through the different heart operations that she underwent. Towards the end of her life all she wanted was to die peacefully with no fuss. Her wish was granted.

I wish my love would cease to flow
And ease the pain within,
To make me forget the love I felt
And help me live again.

I pray each night will erase
The laughter and love we shared,
So that I can forget
How very much I cared.

Months of hopelessness,
Years of fears,
Broken promises, forgotten love,
Floating on lakes of tears.

One wish is all that I need
And that to peacefully die,
For now I am so tired
I cannot even cry.

# 76

# *Nature*

The time spent living in Spain was truly eye-opening, especially when it came to observing nature. From beneath a rock would dart a tiny lizard looking for food or simply wanting to sun himself, and eagles would fly above the mountain tops as though they were constantly on guard. The perfect aroma of herbs, hung in the air tantalising the senses. I couldn't think of a better place to be.

Mountains undulating toward the sea,
where thyme, rosemary, fennel and wild sage grow.

A snake coiled asleep in the heather, a rabbit
tremulous and shy, disappears into a burrow.

A flat rock surface sparkles with droplets
of water, sprayed from a nearby stream.

Lizards sun themselves, occasionally feeding, their
tongues too quick for the human eye to see.

A rolling stone reveals a silent toad looking
with baleful eyes at the intruder.

Its sleep disturbed, it moves slowly from the
light into the rocks a little further.

These mountains, so forbidding from afar,
are alive with every kind of creature.

They harbour them from birth until they
die, the cycle starts again, this is nature.

# 77

# *Inhibitions*

How wonderful it feels when summer arrives and the warmth of the sun allows us to shed our layers of clothes to feel light and free. Even better when we take off our shoes – '*Ahh*,' I hear you say! When we finally shed all our clothes we feel totally vulnerable, shy, defenceless; somehow it hampers the way we think, so very quickly we cover up again to feel safe. How the mind can play tricks on us!

Shed your inhibitions with your clothes,
Free yourself from the eternal prison,
Shed your shoes, take off your hat,
Get rid of bits of this and that,
Feel the texture of your skin
And especially feel the glow within,
For your birthday suit is the best of all,
Walk freely, fearlessly, walk tall.

# 78

# *Even for Love*

Many of Betty's clients visited her for help with their relationships, the most common problem being freedom of thought and deed. Clients would even write and say, 'Don't tell my husband. He will go mad that I have written to you.' We do not have the right to own any other human being. Relationships should be based on trust, freedom of mind and body, and the right to speak our minds even when we know the other party disagrees. We need to unveil a relationship and see its potential and beauty, not stifle it.

No one has the right to
expect a human being to
renounce freedom of
thought and deed and walk
forever in the footsteps
of another, even for love;
to be brainwashed into
believing one is always
wrong is the ultimate sin
and the scars are forever.
The mind should always
remain open to new ideas;
to cling haphazardly to the
past is stifling and corrosive
and will eventually leave its
mark. To love freely without
inhibitions or regrets should
be a way of life and not
something one has served as
a delicacy when the mood prevails;
the decisions we make must be
equally matched with the courage
to fulfil them and to barter the
soul for peace of mind is to
become a traitor to one's own
destiny.

# 79

# *The Willow*

The willow tree was one of Betty's favourites. She loved its small flowers borne on catkins and its pliant branches yielding timber for cricket bats and baskets. Its flexible, supple, graceful and sylph-like form makes it unique amongst trees and inspired Betty to write this beautiful eulogy.

The willow bends
over the river, its leaves
skimming the surface
swirled by the currents
it depends upon for
sustenance, alternately
wet and dry.

The seemingly fragile
branches have a strength
of their own; the trunk
leans with a bearing
neither regal nor submissive,
something difficult
to define. Dignity!

Unlike other trees in
appearance, it has an
individual beauty; shaped
like an umbrella it gives
protection from the
wind and sun to the waterfowl
and their young; they thrive together.

The beavers feed on them,
fell the branches and
dam up tiny streams to
make artificial lakes
where fishes breed;
wherever waters flow,
the willows gather.

# 80

# Stay With Me

*'She bore about with her, she could not help knowing it, the torch of her beauty; she carried it erect into any room that she entered; and after all, veil it as she might, and shrink from the monotony of bearing that it imposed on her, her beauty was apparent. She had been admired. She had been loved.'*

VIRGINIA WOOLF
1882–1941

The novels of Virginia Woolf, such as *Waves* first published in 1931, really captured the attention of Betty. Virginia chose to experiment with the narrative form of writing, which proved to be very successful. Like Betty, she lived in Sussex and both enjoyed the peaceful surroundings of the countryside, enabling them to write prolifically. Unlike Betty, however, Virginia was known to suffer from depression and sadly died on 28 March 1941 – Betty died on 26 March 2002. Both were outstanding writers of their era and both will be remembered for their books for years to come.

Do not go away
Lest my heart stops beating through grief
And the blue skies become as dark as the darkest night;
Do not leave now
Lest my blood run as cold as the ice upon the mountain top
And my love as it overflows freezes into icicles
That reach the ground.

Do not go away
Lest my supple fingers stiffen and turn into claws
And the spring in my walk disappears
Leaving my feet dragging painfully across the floor,
Do not leave me now
For I love you so much
And the pain could not be endured.

# 81

# *Tranquillity*

The ever-changing, rotating universe is dependent on energy waves that create slipstreams, vortices, rivers and seas. The vibrational force never stops and encompasses everything that exists. The best way to live our lives is to go with the flow of energy, stimulating our bodies and minds so that we can become part of the whole. If we are lucky, the universe will let us glimpse the wonders that exist in our dimension.

Streams and mountains
are more peaceful
than the sea where the
crashing waves against
the rocks, and people,
spoil the tranquillity.

Cool streams cascading
gently down from the
heights clean and
sparkle amidst the
flower-strewn fields
in the sunlight.

Trees rustle with
sudden gusts of wind,
no other sounds
disturb the peace.
close to nature and
alone – no longer the
need for pretence.

# 82

# *In Search of You*

Missing children. How terrible it is to see programmes on how children have just disappeared without trace, their photographs displayed across the television screen, distraught parents asking for any information on where their child might be. The pain and sorrow shown disturbs the very core of our hearts, as we learn how the search becomes a neverending task and all bits of information end up in a dead end. Every so often Betty's gifts of clairvoyance would be able to pinpoint where these missing children were, one being the reunion of a daughter with her father all the way from Hong Kong. If only more people could develop this gift, the world would be a happier place.

As the rivers will flow
unceasingly into the distance
to meet the roaring seas
and birds soar uncaringly upon the wing
so will I search this earth
until I find you.

I will walk the valleys
where the silence can be heard
and climb the hills
from dawn till dusk
and ask each passing peasant
to help me, if I must,
for of your love
I have the greatest need.

Without you, the years will pass
and neither the depths nor heights
of living will I achieve,
only the sadness at having
lost you will remain
and the thought that I may
never hold you near again.

# 83

## *Life*

'*Life is a hard fight, a struggle, a wrestling with the principle of evil. Hand to hand, foot to foot. Every inch of the way is disputed. The night is given us to take breath and to pray, to drink deep at the fountain of power. The day, to use the strength which has been given us, to go forth to work with it 'til the evening.*'

FLORENCE NIGHTINGALE
1820–1910

Florence Nightingale, the first woman to nurse British soldiers abroad and instigate the founding of District Nursing, was born a natural healer and was known for her superhuman labours during the Crimean War. It was a life-long continuous effort for her, marked by the reputation of a truly amazing character which has lived and grown and spread to the ends of the earth.

Florence had a powerful mind and she always got to the core of the problem. She and Betty ran parallel with their belief that knowledge is the only way to remedy most of the ills of mankind. It is said that Florence Nightingale's voice had magical powers of rare character; this Betty had too. In one rare recording of Florence's made in 1890 she says, '*When I am no longer even a memory, just a name, I hope my voice may perpetuate the great work of my life.*' Betty and Florence will be heard across the world for many years to come.

Walk into the night, into the darkness
That folds like a cloak
Around the path already trodden.

Walk fearlessly along the tangly track
Dismissing fears that creep
Into the mind unbidden.

Let not the hollow noises
Of the unknown deter you.
Go steadily along your course.

Walk into the night, unafraid,
Follow the vibrant stream of life
Until you find its source.

# 84

# *Memories*

Where would we be without memories? Beautiful, happy memories enhance our lives, for we learn from them and turn negative into positive. Memories are a lifeline, especially at a time when we may feel down.

Recall a happy memory every day to ensure a bright future.

I shall remember this summer
when the icy fingers of winter
whiten the trees and the grass
is no longer green.

The gentle way you held my hand,
the moisture of your kiss
and the smile in your eyes
when you teased.

The memories are mine
they can never be erased,
forever you will always
be a part of me.

# 85

# *My Wish*

In this most personal of poems, Betty expressed the wish to soak up every ray of sunshine and to rest in a peaceful place among nature and loved ones. This wish was granted to her.

Don't bury me
In soggy damp clay,
That in a short time
Will rot me away.

Bury me where
The sun beats down;
Beneath the dry
And warming ground.

Where my body
Will slowly dry;
And the gentle rain,
For me, will cry.

# LYRICS

# 86

# Music Set in Stone

In Betty's very own words:
*'You have to keep the imperfections to survive in this imperfect world, so don't change a thing.'*

The most fantastic gift that music gives us is that it never dies – the tune and words are remembered for ever. When recorded, music transmits itself back to us with powerful energy. It is well known that the first attempt at playing a piece of music or singing a song is usually the best, as we perform it in an unadulterated way, in its purest form. Music is cast like a piece of sculpture and remains for ever in our memory.

When the music is set in stone,
It can't be changed,
Because we've chosen the notes, and the key,
And the words are in place
For the melody.

We spent so many hours
Composing the tune,
But all too soon
You have your doubts
Of what it's all about

Don't waste my time,
Make up your mind,
But I'm telling you,
If you change anything
It won't be the same.

When it's set in stone,
It can't be changed,
We've chosen the notes, and the key,
And the words are in place
For the melody.

If you want us to sing the same tune,
Just leave it alone
And let's set it in stone.

# 87

# The World Keeps Turning

'Life goes on' as the saying goes. We can all relate to that. When all is said and done, we must continue living and growing spiritually, even through the bad times in our lives, hoping that one day we will see the light into the next dimension.

I know the world can't stand still
Can't stop turning,
So I'm learning to live again,
Willing myself not to cry,
To get it into my head
That a part of my heart isn't dead.

Because I know you're around
Although I can't see you
You made me so proud
And I believed you
When the last time you left
You told me not to forget
You'd love me forever.

So I'm hoping one day
That I will see you
And I will pray
That the gods will be kind
And we'll be together sometime
Perhaps we'll share a dream.

I'm going to get it together
However long it takes
And hope the world
Becomes a better place
Than it's ever been before
I can't ask for more

I know you're around
Although I can't see you
You made me so proud
And I believed you
When the last time you left
You told me not to forget
You'd love me forever.
And then you were gone
But I know we still belong
Together.

# 88

## *One By One*

'*We are not here just to survive and live long We are here to live and know life in its multi-dimensions, to know life in its richness, in all its variety. And when a man lives multi-dimensionally, explores all possibilities available, never shrinks back from any challenge, goes, rushes to it, welcomes it, rises to the occasion then life becomes a flame, life blooms.*'

BHAGWAN SHREE RAJNEESH
1931–1990

As the years went by, like most of us Betty began to lose the loved ones dear to her. The first person was her father when she was just eleven, a man who was admired for his intelligence and wit. Then Betty's mother passed away, a woman of trememdous warmth and humour who welcomed people with open arms into her home. And so her family and friends began to disappear. Like all families they could be quite difficult at times; none the less Betty missed them all and longed to meet up with them again in spirit. Now I know she has.

One by one
I have lost the dear ones close to me
Old familiar faces I can still recall.
I took for granted all the things that mattered most to me
Then one day suddenly
I looked around and found I'd lost them all.

So hold me close don't ever say goodbye my love
Because without you my life would have no reason.
Your smiling face will chase away the heartaches
One by one
But love will stay through every changing season.

One by one
We will fill our nights and days with love
Life is just beginning now that you are near.
In lonely moments when old memories come back to me
We'll kiss and suddenly all my loneliness will disappear.

So hold me close don't ever say goodbye my love
Because without you my life would have no reason.
Your smiling face will chase away the heartaches
One by one
But love will stay through every changing season.

So hold me close
Let's take the years
One by one.

# 89

## *Take It Easy*

None of us take enough 'time out' for ourselves. Rushing from A to B, filling our lives with constant activity, we need to stop and reflect on how we are feeling inside. Yoga exercise and relaxation are a marvellous tool for slowing down the mind and body, being aware of the breath and the energy within. Hard at first, I know, but gradually you will feel tremendous benefits and you will re-learn how to *take it easy*!

Take it easy –
That's what life's all about,
It's not a race against time.
It's about the moments
That we don't plan
When time stands still
And you hold the world in your hands.

Look, but don't try to explore,
Take one day at a time.
For the love you seek is closer to home,
That's where you'll find it,
I know!

There will be times
When clouds darken the sky,
But if you're laid back
You can say, 'Take it easy–
There's plenty of time
I can sit and wait 'til it clears.'

And then you'll thank God
That you have survived
And for the rest of your life
You can say, 'Take it easy –
There's plenty of time
Because I'm here to stay.'

# 90

# *Attitude*

This was a lyric written for all those who have continuously been put down by others throughout their lives. We often hear people comment, 'You haven't got the right attitude to your work,' or 'You have an attitude.' We need to have a particular frame of mind to survive in life and having 'attitude' can be a very positive quality, as long as it is constructive and not destructive.

The lyrics here were written by Betty with music by Adam Leclercq, a talented musician who worked with care, sensitivity and passion on all the lyrics shown in this book. I am sure if you get to hear it you will love his interpretation.

Attitude, I have attitude,
And you're can't complain,
'Cos you're to blame,
You never liked my style.

The way I walked,
The way I talked.
Nothing was right,
So overnight,
I got attitude.

Now I strut my stuff,
And it feels so good,
As I walk along
The road, alone.

There's no one to whine
About my mind,
I can play the fool
And drink the wine.

You'll never know
How great it feels,
Now that you're
No longer around.

I can walk, and talk,
And strut my stuff.
And it feels great,
And I can't wait
To get more attitude.

# 91

# *Hold Back the Night*

When we have something good, whether a person or an experience, we want to hold on to it, never letting it go in case we lose it forever. Children cling on to their parents, lovers walk arm entwined around arm – we seem to want and need this closeness more than anything else. We want to make the day last, pushing back time so that the enjoyment of another person's company lingers on into the night. 'Hold back the night' was a lyric loved by Betty as it reflected totally her own emotions.

Hold back the night
I want to touch your face again,
For when it's light you disappear from view,
The mists roll in, we part, and have to wait too long
Until I feel your touch and know you're back with me.

The dreams we share are not a fantasy,
We're in a space that no one else can see.
We don't exist in daylight hours,
So when I wake, I want to close my eyes again,
To feel you close, to touch your face,
To know you're near.

The dreams we share are not a fantasy,
We're in a space that no one else can see.
So please close all the doors, shut out the light
And let's –
Hold back the night.

# 92

# Take Your Time

*Do not walk through*
*Time*
*Without evidence*
*Of your passage.*

POPE JOHN XXIII
1881–1963

Each one of us at some time makes a rash decision, either because we are angry or because we just can't wait until the time is right. It is very difficult to look at our actions from a distance and see that we are perhaps wrong. It takes others to coax and persuade us to stay around for a little while longer – if we are lucky enough to have someone who cares and will take time to look after us.

How I wish you weren't leaving,
Even the stars are grieving.
What should have been a moonlit night
Is dark, because they've lost their light,
And in the day the colours turn to grey
Because I'm losing you today.

Perhaps you won't find it easy,
When the time comes to leave,
Every step we have taken
Was planned to make
A host of memories.
So, take your time.

We were always two, never one,
It's not the same for everyone.
How can you crumble walls of stone
That we built – that we own –
And have them disappear from sight?
You don't have the right.

Take your time –
You won't find it easy,
When the time comes to leave,
Every step we have taken
Was planned to make
A host of memories.

If you decide to change your mind
I know that you would find
That building all the walls again
Would help erase the pain,
And we'd discover the love we found
The first time around.

# 93

# Lady of the Night

This is a fantastic lyric written by Betty at a time when she was brimming over with ideas. It conjures up a sense of mystery, an unobtainable dream. Every desire we have remains in our heart until it is fulfilled. These desires consist of energies that can make or break us, so when you have an unobtainable dream, enjoy it while you can and then let it drift away. Always move forward with your life.

Sophisticated, feline lady, you're the one for me
Walking, talking, cat-like stalking, I can hardly breathe.
I can't believe I've never seen you, only in my dreams,
So stay awhile, don't walk away, there may not be a day
That leads into another night like this.

My dream was just a fantasy, but you are my reality.
You must believe I'll never see the like of you again.
Let me stay, don't walk away, lead me, please don't leave me
Until it's light, my lady of the night,

Many times I've walked this way looking at the moon,
Hoping it would make my dreams come true.
Feline features lit by lamplight, eyes of green, so mean and cat-like,
Reason tells me I should walk away. To hell with reason,
I am going to stay; having seen you I'll not walk away.

My dream was just a fantasy, but you are my reality.
You must believe I'll never see the like of you again.
Let me stay, don't walk away, lead me, please don't leave me
Until it's light, my lady of the night.

I'm going down the road to where? I've no idea and I don't care.
The promise in your eyes and smile will make me stay around awhile
Until the moment you decide to walk into the night again,
My walking, talking, cat-like stalking friend.

# 94

# My Life's a Travesty

Like the ever-changing faces on the walls, you too will change.
There will be light in your eyes, you will be at ease with yourself.
Nurturing natural gifts will help you to achieve the impossible dream.
Our mind is everlasting; we must be earthed so that we can fly. We
think that miracles only happen to others – one will happen to you
that you will treasure for ever.

From time to time I think my life's a travesty
When everything is not quite what it seems.
Trying to smile when I'm feeling low
Isn't easy, no not easy, so I know
I'll have to think about it, how to begin,
Have to learn how to win,
Then maybe, just maybe, find me.

I'm going to get up off the ground
Try walking on air.
Who wants a life of misery
If I can save my sanity
When I could be a lighter,
And oh so much brighter,
A lighter, brighter, happier me?

The secret, I know, is not so much a mystery
But knowing how to recognise the signs
When the highs become the lows.
It isn't easy, no not easy, but I know
I'll try much harder than ever before,
Now that I know the score
And I know I'm going to succeed.

I'm going to get up off the ground
Try walking on air.
Who wants a life of misery
If I can save my sanity
When I could be lighter,
And oh so much brighter,
A lighter, brighter, happier me?

# 95

# Ghosts of the Past

*Having opened*
*The door of hope*
*I know my spirit*
*Will soar and*
*Untold wonders will*
*Be revealed.*

BETTY SHINE
1929–2002

This poem is about the days when Betty was an opera singer. It was her great passion in life to stand on stage and feel the energy of the audience. At the peak of her career she was offered the opportunity to tour around the world as a top star, performing with her operatic heroes and being recognised for the amazing voice that she had. But it was not meant to be. It would have meant leaving her family and children for six months of the year, and she just could not find it in her heart to do that, so her dream was shattered. Betty went on to become one of the most famous personalities in her field and a brilliant writer, but she never lost the desire to work again in the theatre.

I'm not playing tonight
Because they've turned out the lights
For the last time.
There's no performance,
No audience, no atmosphere;
It's sad, because I loved being here.

This place
Is where I learnt my trade
And made all my mistakes.
And learnt the meaning of fear
When I heard the words
It's time for you to appear.

Now, I'm speaking my lines in the dark,
And in the silence I hear
The ghosts of the past.
So I'm staying behind
With my own kind
Because my spirit is here.

This place
Is where I learnt my trade
And made all my mistakes.
And learnt the meaning of fear
When I heard the words
It's time for you to appear.
So I'm staying behind
With my own kind
Because my spirit is here.

# 96

# *Ambition*

Ambition is a word we all use in our vocabulary – but do we fully understand the meaning? A desire to advance ourselves, to achieve our ultimate goal – but along with ambition we can build a barrier around ourselves, not being able to see when perhaps we are treading on someone else's toes for our own advancement. Opportunities are there for us all, but not at the price of losing self respect. By all means have ambition, but know the boundaries and stick to them. You will be thankful in the end.

There's a river running through my mind
That pays no heed to tides or time
And when it meets an estuary
It flows into the sea.
I never know from day to day
Where it's taking me.

I was ripe, I'd arrived,
I never cared when others cried.
Ambition was a god to me,
I designed my destiny.
How wrong can one man be?

I've lived my life on borrowed time,
I couldn't wait to stand in line,
Enjoy the well-earned limelight–
A kind of shallow life.
Now I can clearly see
It's pay back time for me.

I was ripe, I'd arrived,
I never cared when others cried.
Ambition was a god to me,
I designed my destiny.
How wrong can one man be?

When I couldn't stop the course
I knew I had to find the source,
And it led back to me.
Only I could stop the flow,
So now I've finally let go
To stem the tides of time.

I was ripe, I'd arrived,
I never cared when others cried.
Ambition was a god to me,
How wrong could one man be
When I designed my destiny?

# 97

# *Visions*

Betty wrote this last lyric from deep within her soul, demonstrating she was a true visionary. After completing this song, she wrote a note explaining how she felt:

'*I don't like looking into the future too much (I try to live my life one day at a time). I don't know what is going to happen to all the poems and lyrics I have written, but I feel something big is going to happen, so we will just have to wait and see and stay with it until they [the spirit helpers] care to enlighten us! All this material I have written will reach the public when the time is right and when it will have the optimum impact. That could be anytime from now, going on a couple of years – let's hope it's sooner rather than later!*

'*This particular period has given me so much pleasure it has actually lifted me up when I thought I couldn't take any more. So I thank those who helped me and for bringing the poetry, lyrics and music together. This has been a masterstroke for me in every way.*'

Visions I have seen
Are embossed with very special scenes,
Like the candles in the sky
And the shifting tides of light
That change to coloured rays.
Some I've never seen before
And may not see again.

From deep within the folds of golden tapestry
Notes made of crystal tears emerge,
Moving back and forth
To conjure up the chords
Of music that is never heard
Outside the confines of this night
That's lit by candlelight.

I have never seen,
And may never see again,
The wonder of these scenes
Separated from humanity,
Until someone sees the light
On a very special night.

Too often I have heard,
The scathing tones of those
Who mock the beauty of the light,
And scenes they cannot see
Because they have a darker side
That they cannot hide.

But they have never seen
The silver threads
That hang above my head
Reminiscent of a spider's web
And the beauty of simplicity
In the ever-changing energies
That separate for some
Levels that are rarely seen
In these shifting scenes.

I have never seen,
And may never see again,
This beauty and simplicity.
But I won't forget
The colours and the music of this night,
And scenes that touched my soul
That were lit by candlelight.

# FINAL THOUGHTS

# 98

## *It's a Mystery*

Life, both this one and the next, will always remain a mystery. We can only speculate about what happens to us when we die. Betty took great comfort from what she herself experienced and helped the bereaved and terminally ill conquer their fears. She wrote:

*'My own meditation has taken me into realms of tranquillity and love beyond all comprehension in this world.'*

It's difficult to comprehend
Exactly where our journey ends.
Is there a world that we can't see,
Where we meet, where we speak
To those we've loved and lost?

And do we really see a light
That takes us to a greater height
Outside the realms of gravity
Where we can clarify our dreams?

How can we define the thoughts
We have inside our minds
That affect all humankind?
Maybe, it's best to wait and see
What's behind the mystery.

# 99

# *Without You*

Hope is eternal – without it we are lost. No single word or one particle of energy is ever wasted. Remember the visible is only a minute part of the invisible.

The words of this lyric express totally the feelings I have about losing Betty. Betty always said we had invisible wings and can fly to eternity if we so desire. I am sure there were sides to Betty's great character that were yet to unfold and be discovered and I only wish I had had more time to experience them with her. Life is certainly very empty without Betty's physical presence, especially her infectious laughter and her continuous thirst for new adventures. Her presence will be felt for ever.

We have so little time to waste,
The world is such an empty place
Without you.

I want to walk with you and fly with you,
I want to laugh and cry with you,
I want to see the other sides of you
I haven't seen before. Because life's no fun
Without you.

And you must know the music that we made
We can make again, because I have the score.
And the wealth you brought cannot be bought
'Cos I don't want to be without you any more.

I want to walk with you and fly with you,
To see the other sides of you,
And see again the shady lanes
We walked when our love was new.

Do you remember the colour
of the autumn leaves, from trees of every shade?
And when we crushed them all beneath our feet
And laughed until we cried at that stupid game?

I've no appetite for loneliness
I must confess, so let's sing the song
from the score within my heart,
And make music, as we did before.
And never part. Because I can't fly
Without you.

# 100

# *A Web of Dreams*

*To Betty with Love from her grand-daughter Raina*

Betty is my best friend. She was and is one of the most honest and caring people I have met and is a big part of my life. I talk of her as being here because I truly believe that she is with me. When I ask her for help if I'm feeling down she shows me a sign that she is there. I feel her presence often and she gives me the strength to carry on. I can still hear her laughter, her humour – she gives me enthusiasm for life just as she did when she was here on earth. Betty and I spent many times together chatting, laughing and listening to one another's problems! We had so many interests in common, music, books, the news, the human condition and nature. I would spend many hours in her lovely conservatory which looked out on to the garden and bird table. She loved watching the birds feed.

I always thought of Betty as a 21 year old, her mind was so vibrant and she was full of energy and warmth. As her grand-daughter, she would always want to know what I was doing, and was especially interested in my boyfriends! My mother Janet, Betty and me were always called the trio! We would go out for meals, go to the theatre, spend time shopping and having cups of coffee. When we three starting talking, no one else could get a word in edge-ways!

I would like to tell Betty through this book that I love her with all my heart. I know there will be many times that we will still be able to share. I know you are being looked after, Betty, by those above that love you. *A Web of Dreams* is my favourite poem.

Love
Raina

A web of silver threads
Reflect our dreams
As they are caught in ribbons
Of soft moonbeams.

The magic of the moon
Is there for all to see,
But they cannot solve
It's mystery.

Only on these nights
Can we choose
The shadows or the light,
For the kind of life we want to live
To make our dreams come true.

A web of silver threads
And soft moonbeams
Light up the darkest night
And hold the key
To its mystery.

# 101

# The Brightest Star

In every sense of the word Betty was a *Star*. Shining more brightly and radiantly than anyone I have ever known, she showed love and compassion to all who knew her. What a huge personality too – her unique laughter was recognised by everyone! She overcame the obstacles that were put in her way with great determination and positivity, and her life from beginning to end was full of amazing talent. Yes, like us all she fell many times, and at these times my heart would be broken for her. I could not bear to see her hurt in any way. The mother/daughter bond was and is so strong we were always there for each other, no matter what happened. The inspiration that Betty gave to us all was immeasurable and I will for ever be in her debt for the true unconditional love she gave.

Bless you Betty. Bless you Mum.

There is no moon,
No melodies
When you're not around.
Only the dark
Of the darkest nights
And hollow sounds
That make no sense
When you're absent.

You were, you are,
The brightest star of all,
And I the one who saw you fall.
Like every object bright,
You lit up my nights.

Shallow I may be,
And selfish, yes,
But you were loved by me
And I will have no rest
Until the moon returns
Along with the stars.

Then the sounds
Will not be hollow at all
But the whisperings of a past
That was full of love
And could be full of love again.

You were, you are,
The brightest star of all,
And I the one who saw you fall.
Like every object bright,
You lit up my nights,
And life makes no sense
When you're absent.

# Index

If you wish to purchase the new CD that features some of the lyrics in this book, please write to the address below:

Janet Shine
P.O. Box 1009
Hassocks
West Sussex
BN6 8XS

Other tapes and books are also available at the above address. Please enclose a stamped addressed envelope for a reply. Thank you.

*By the same author*

# MY LIFE AS A MEDIUM
## An Autobiography

Betty Shine has been a world famous medium for over 20 years and is highly respected for her remarkable powers and healing skills. Her extraordinary gifts have touched many hearts and inspired the lives of thousands of people from all walks of life. Yet, in spite of being guided by spirit voices from the age of two, Betty Shine admits she was initially reluctant to accept her personal destiny.

This is Betty's compelling story, describing an incredible personal journey from a career as an opera singer into the world of alternative healing and her poignant struggle to come to terms with her powerful gifts. In it, she shares some of the truly amazing and inspirational encounters she has experienced along the way, including astral travel, near death experiences, clairvoyant medical diagnosis and her discovery and study of Mind Energy.

'Betty's wisdom, down-to-earth attitude and sense of humour come across clearly through the pages of this book.'      *Psychic News*

ISBN 0-00-653138-5

# A MIND OF YOUR OWN

## A Book for Life

*A Mind of Your Own* is a sourcebook for the millennium. Although the world changes around us, human beings never change – we experience the same thoughts, emotions and problems generation after generation.

In this book, Betty Shine uses over 200 carefully selected keywords to identify the most common anxieties which face people today – and then, drawing on her 20 years' experience of working as a medium and healer, she demonstrates how to overcome them. Now *you* can harness the potential of your own mind to improve your life and the lives of those around you.

Widely acclaimed as the most significant work of Betty Shine's long and distinguished career, *A Mind of Your Own* is a book both to read and to dip into. Nobody – from the ardent believer to the most hardened sceptic – can fail to be touched by the magic and the wisdom shared in this highly personal and deeply powerful book. It holds the power to change your life.

'Those who encounter Betty Shine's supernatural powers find it hard to remain sceptical'                    *Independent*

ISBN 0-00-653019-2

*By the same author*

# THE INFINITE MIND
## The Mind/Brain Phenomenon

In the 25 years that Betty Shine has studied Mind Energy, the force that she herself discovered, the world of science has grown up. But scientists always make the same mistake; they fail to distinguish between the physical grey matter, the Brain, and the wonderful source of life itself, the Mind.

*The Infinite Mind* presents the proof for the existence of the Mind independent of the biological functions of the Brain. Drawing on a wide range of remarkable personal stories about survival evidence and contact with coma patients, including those involving celebrities from the worlds of entertainment and football, Betty Shine's irre-futable evidence and observations will inspire individuals from all walks of life to re-examine their beliefs.

'Betty is funny and warm, and there is nothing superhuman about her manner. But some of the things she takes for granted would send shivers down the normal spine.'                      *Daily Mail*

ISBN 0-00-653104-0

# A FREE SPIRIT
## Gives You the Right to Make Choices

A lifetime of healing has given Betty Shine an insight into the inhumanity that prevails in today's society. The interaction between every living thing on this planet affects us all, and so many life forms have become extinct that it is only a matter of time before it could happen to us.

There is a way out, and that is for everyone who cares about our planet to take up the challenges represented in this book. With courage and tenacity you can become a Free Spirit. Whether an animal lover or simply seeking to improve your relationships, this book will give you a simple philosophy that could change your life.

In *A Free Spirit*, Betty Shine not only shares her own remarkable gifts but also recalls the experiences of her readers when their own healing abilities have been revealed at the time they needed them most. You will be inspired by Betty's relentless campaign against cruelty, both in the animal kingdom and our own, but her greatest gift to you will be the key to the doors of your mind that would otherwise remain closed.

ISBN 0-00-653203-9

*By the same author*

# THE LITTLE BOOK OF COSMIC COLOUR

## Secrets of Colour Healing, Harmony and Therapy

**Feeling grey? You need colour!**

*The Little Book of Cosmic Colour* is a pocket companion to energize and heal you. By using appropriate colour at different times, you can bring balance and harmony to your life.

Betty Shine is the world's leading healer. In this little book she shares the secrets of using colour to stimulate your senses and emotions, heal ailments and improve your confidence. She also shows how to 'feel' invisible auras and how to use colour more effectively in the home, at work, and in what you wear.

'I am quite convinced that she has certain remarkable powers'
*Mail on Sunday*

ISBN 0-00-653200-4